Culture in the Plural

Culture in the Plural

michel de certeau

Edited and with an Introduction by Luce Giard

Translated and with an Afterword by Tom Conley

University of Minnesota Press

Minneapolis

London

The University of Minnesota Press gratefully acknowledges
financial assistance provided by the French Ministry of Culture for
the translation of this book.

Originally published as *La culture au pluriel,* © 1974 Union Générale d'Éditions.
Nouvelle édition établie et présentée par Luce Giard, © 1994 Éditions du Seuil.

Published by the University of Minnesota Press
111 Third Avenue South, Suite 290
Minneapolis, MN 55401-2520

http://www.upress.umn.edu
Second printing 2001
Printed in the United States of America on acid-free paper

Library of Congress Cataloging-in-Publication Data

Certeau, Michel de.
    [Culture au pluriel. English]
    Culture in the plural / Michel de Certeau ; edited and with an
introduction by Luce Giard ; translated and with an afterword by Tom
Conley.
      p.   cm.
    Includes index.
    ISBN 0-8166-2766-5 (hc : alk. paper). — ISBN 0-8166-2767-3 (pb :
alk. paper)
    1. Culture. 2. Multiculturalism. 3. Language and culture.
4. Political culture. I. Giard, Luce. II. Title.
HM101.C4213   1998
306—dc21   97-25361

Contents

Contents

Preface

These studies on culture lead to a "conclusion" that might well be their introduction. Their collation has been constructed on the basis of this terminal point. The final perspectives indicate the way I should like to redeploy all these works for new tasks and other battles. The surge of the current stage back over those that have prepared it constitutes this very book.

It was born of common investigations and conversations whose form, at least in one case, is explicitly of a dialogue. It includes an article that was coauthored by Dominique Julia, Jacques Revel, and myself.[1] I would like to put the articles as a whole under the sign of this plural writing. This work aims at a disappropriation of culture at the same time as a passage toward signifying practices (or productive operations). It goes in the direction of an eradication of propriety and of the proper name. This path leads us — without myself being able to get there — toward the anonymous seas in which creativity murmurs a violent song. Creation comes from origins further removed than its authors, ostensible subjects, and exceeds their works, objects whose closure is fictive. Something indeterminate is articulated in these indeterminations. All forms of differentiation refer each place to a labor of its other. This labor, more essential than its backgrounds or its representations, is *culture*.

[1974]

What has become of a book six years later? Footprints still left and landscapes crossed. Since then, other investigations have given way to *The Practice of Everyday Life,* which no longer deals with scholarly, popular or marginal, imaginary or political forms of culture, but the operativity and virtuosity of ordinary practices, the countless dynamics of daily activities. It is perhaps a passage from the "plural" to the multiple, and from social figures to the moving ground that they bring into view.

Here and there a few questions inhabit these travels in the foreign lands that compose a society. It would be more exact to say that they haunt these labors, for it is uncertain that these investigations can be taken up in any direct way. I especially wonder about the relations that networks of *operations* maintain with fields of *credibility*. Far from having these networks and fields constitute coherent systems, everything leads one to believe, to the contrary, that a Brownian movement of practices crisscrosses through and through all social strata, piled up like a tuff, often broken and mixed, whose institutions partially guarantee the equilibrium and give way to management. From then on, it must be asked how a combination of forces in competition or conflict develops a multitude of tactics in spaces organized at once through constraints and through contracts.

This volume deals especially with cultural institutions that form only one of the instances of activity "at work" in a social hierarchy. But it is already framed by the examination of two other instances: the one comes under the jurisdiction of *an anthropology of credibility*, of its displacements and metamorphoses from the so-called superstitions up to the sciences or to the media; the other is to envisage *ways of doing* — good tricks, sleights of hand, everyday ruses — in a *tactical science* (or "logic"). The work sites are open.

If, in every society, games make clear the formality of its practices for the reason that, outside of the conflicts of everyday life, it no longer has to be concealed, then the old game of hopscotch becomes a kind of map in which, on a series of places and according to a sum of rules, a social *art* unfolds a field of play in order to create itineraries, and to make use of the surprises that lie ahead. It is a scale model, a theoretical fiction. In effect, culture can be compared to this art, conditioned by places, rules, and givens; it is a proliferation of inventions in limited spaces.

[1980]

Introduction
Opening the Possible
Luce Giard

A historian of early modern Europe (a period ranging from the sixteenth to the seventeenth century), Michel de Certeau studied with predilection questions of religion and the experience of mystics, in a time of turmoil in which the Christian tradition was being fractured into rival churches, when the most lucid minds witnessed a fading of the signs of God, when they were reduced to seeking in the secrets of inner adventure the certitude of a divine presence that elsewhere, outside, could no longer be grasped.[1] From this process of emancipation, Certeau investigated with respect and with an astonishing tact the obscure paths — not in order to hierarchize them, nor to designate the factions belonging to truth and the right way, but to learn from the past how a social group traverses the desertion of its beliefs and how it might profit from the conditions to which it is subjected in order to invent its liberty and plot out a space of movement.

Certeau had constituted this style of reading cultural and social history at the intersections of disciplines and methods, associating the concepts and procedures of philosophy, linguistics, and psychoanalysis with history and anthropology. Far from searching for a convenient eclecticism or a conciliatory syncretism, he wanted to grasp each historical moment in the multiplicity of its constituent parts and in the contradiction of its conflicts. He defied the anachronistic superimposition of grids that map our knowledge onto past societies. With *The Writing of History* (1975), a new and demanding reflection on the epistemology of history, he made himself known to the historical tribe that had already taken notice of his dossier on *La Possession de Loudun* (1970). In these two works he equally showed how the historian always produces the writing of history from the standpoint of the present, from his or her relation with governing powers, from questions for which a social group needs to seek an answer and that, for lack of other solutions, it transposes on the past in order to keep at a distance or exorcise the dangers of the present.

With history understood in this way, it is hardly surprising that Certeau associated his first works with a point of observation and clarification dedicated to the present, to the obstacles of our own society. In a way, he had come to this second area of research in May 1968, under the pressure of circumstances; at that time the editor of *Études*, a monthly review of culture published by the Society of Jesus (of which he was a member), he had accompanied and commented on the "events," as they were then described, in a series of articles written in the heat of the moment, and assembled in the following autumn in a small book titled *La prise de parole* [*The Capture of Speech*], whose highly personal tone and perspicacity were soon to become legendary.[2] The renown of these articles would soon lead to numerous invitations to collaborate in different projects, in different areas of reflection and consultation. He thus accompanied social workers, directors of cultural centers, but also managers who, at the Commission on Planning or in the entourage of different ministries, were pondering the future evolution of French society.

These meetings, these labors, and these experiences constituted for Certeau many opportunities to deepen and broaden his own reflections, to cast aside both hasty and vague generalities and the clichés that had long served as official doctrine in cultural action. He sought to look deeper and further, hoping to understand whence a society draws its substance of intelligence and fantasy. He never ceased repeating that a cultural or political action, if it is inventive and anchored in reality, cannot be born of a deficit of thinking or be nourished by the contempt of others. He defied the widespread view that caused social and cultural action to be conceived as a beneficial rain of bread crumbs falling off the tables of the knowing and powerful onto the popular classes. He was no less convinced that neither invention nor creativity belongs to professional specialists and that, from anonymous practitioners to famous artists, a thousand abstract networks generate a give-and-take of information and assure these exchanges, without which a society eventually suffocates and dies.

Certeau formulated the reflection along a parallel track with all of these encounters in a series of articles, published between 1968 and 1973, that were initially assembled in the first edition of this volume (in 1974). The whole dealt with social life and the insertion of culture in this life. But what did he mean by this ambiguous term "culture"? This question stands at the center of the book. We need only listen to his response: "If culture is really going to exist, it is not enough to be the author of social practices; these social practices need to have meaning for those who effectuate them" (chapter 5); for culture "consists not in receiving, but in positing the act by which each individual *marks* what others furnish for the needs of living and thinking" (ibid.). From that point on, we are far from the condescending division between a culture of knowledge to be diffused and a popular culture to be studied from a slightly superior angle, in the way we repeat "children's words" without attaching much importance to them. But we are also at an equal distance from an exchange of cultural goods that would place "good people" in the passive consumption of available commodities.

In Certeau's perspective, every culture appeals to an activity, to a mode of appropriation, to a personal accounting and transformation, an exchange instilled in a social group. It is exactly this kind of "staging of culture," if I may say so, that gives shape to each epoch. "Between a society and its scientific models, between a historical situation and the intellectual tools that belong to it, there exists a relation that constitutes a cultural system" (chapter 7). Understood thus, culture is neither a treasure to protect from the ravages of time nor a "sum of values to defend." It simply connotes "a labor to be undertaken over the entire expanse of social life" (chapter 8). It is at once much less (if reference is made to the idea of patrimony) and much more (if we attend to contemporary social activity proclaimed by the adulators of "cultivated culture"). That so many affirmations have their origin in a historian who specialized in the sixteenth and seventeenth centuries and in the Baroque age, broken off from the subtleties of the art of persuasion in the Renaissance, could only irritate or be relegated to the rank of impertinence or other improprieties due to the continued evils of May 1968. Nothing was spared in this regard.

Taken up with vigorously casting aside the expected celebration of "culture in the singular" (of which he underlined how much it always betrays the *singularity of a milieu* in chapter 9), Certeau hardly took notice. Hence his wish to see this culture in the singular, which "always imposes the law of a power," replaced by another conception, based on "culture in the plural," which endlessly makes an appeal to battle (chapter 10).

The voyage from one way of seeing things to the other begins with this observation: there exists a crisis of representations that undermines authority; words that were formerly effective "can no longer be believed because they neither open closed doors nor change things" (chapter 8). The first chapter makes the point clear. Every representation articulates and makes manifest a conviction, which in turn provides a basis for the legitimacy of authority. At the point where belief no longer inhabits representations, authority is bereft of its basis, and is soon deserted. Its power collapses, undermined from within. If, for its part, chapter 3[3] disqualifies the received notion of "popular culture," it is by showing that it was the product of a construction with a political agenda: in the nineteenth century, everyone agreed in praising the innocence and the freshness of popular culture all the more in that its death was what was being sought. The chapter ends on a melancholy note on this obvious point: "Doubtless, there must always be a death for there to be speech." In the memory of the celebrants, nothing can erase the "beauty of the dead."

On a more optimistic note, chapter 4 suggests that universities become "a laboratory that produces a popular culture by proportioning methods to questions and to needs," but it remarks that universities eagerly take refuge in a more familiar task, in which "it becomes a filter that opposes a 'discipline' to pressures exerted from the outside." In order to become other, a prerequisite requirement would have to be satisfied: producing this culture in an idiom that is not foreign to the greater number, something that cannot be thought in a milieu in which the vaguest impulse to simplify orthography brings forth a deluge of protests from all sides — "orthography is an orthodoxy of the past" (chapter 5), always ready to unleash shock troops to defend "the treasure of the French language."[4]

In reading this book almost twenty years after its first edition, we are assured that the objects it studies remain central to our concerns, even if our ways of staging them have changed somewhat. For the most part, the content of the analyses has withstood the test of time; the thinking retains all of its vigor and the style all of its incisiveness. Sometimes, now and again, a word erupts that has lost its familiarity. The written language is also influenced by the effects of style; words are imposed as if by their very nature for a certain time, in certain contexts of thought, on the basis of a certain body of writings. Thus it is, on several occasions, a question of "repression," a term familiar to the actors in the theater of May 1968: "the social function —

that is, above all repressive—of learned culture" is summoned in chapter 3.[5] Later, in chapter 7, the word returns with emphasis in reference to Herbert Marcuse, who himself borrowed the term from Freud, in a filiation that Certeau recalls and discusses.

More than the intensive use of an expression that has since been forgotten, more than the allusions to social expressions once known by everyone, such as the Lip negotiations,[6] the date of these pages is avowed through the mention of two elements structuring social life, but whose role has considerably changed. First of all, there is everything that is related to "labor," even if the issue concerns the social status of labor in urban areas (chapter 2) or the 1968 desire to eradicate "the *isolated* category of the student or the professor" for the purpose of abolishing "the social division of labor" (chapter 4). It is clear that Certeau was writing in the context of a fully employed society, when it was all the easier to clearly denounce alienation in labor in that the latter was available to everyone.

In the same way, when he analyzes the situation in the schools (chapter 5), or that of minorities and their regional cultures (chapter 6), Certeau alludes on several occasions to the decisive action of the unions: it was true at a time when, with the help of full employment, a small number of well-organized labor unions could almost negotiate as equals with the political authorities, but it is no longer the case because of economic recession and the erosion of the credibility of labor unions. The crisis of representations, for which Certeau offered a diagnosis in other areas of social life, has since affected union activities.

Another instance of the difference in the contexts is evident when Certeau discusses violence (chapter 3) in reference to the Third World, to revolutionary struggles, to wars of independence, or when he refers to Vietnam and Chile. Today we think of "ethnic violence" or struggles between factions, of the former Yugoslavia drenched in bloodshed, of Somalia, of the assassinations of Algerian intellectuals, of the endless plight of the Palestinians. In this chapter, Certeau speaks of violence in Hegelian terms, a first way of expressing what will subsequently find its place and pertinence in social conflicts; today, this Hegelian vocabulary would be replaced by the question of anomie and the despair of "excluded" subjects.

Without denying the traces of the style of a given period, we can nonetheless feel a strange swiftness that accompanies an "intelligence without...fear, without fatigue, and without pride,"[7] a mind that moves all over the social map with an astonishing curiosity, and with a secret tenderness for the anonymous crowd. In its own fashion, detached from all partisanship, this book is basically a *political text*, a lesson of liberty. "Politics does not assure happiness, nor does it give meaning to things. It creates or it refuses conditions of possibility. It prohibits or it allows; it makes possible or impossible" (chapter 8). Such was the desire that animated Michel de Certeau throughout his life: *opening possibilities*, managing a space of movement out of which a liberty could be resurgent. History teaches us that the most difficult resource to mobilize is that of beginnings. It seems to me that these lucid and incisive studies today make this force of beginning, this first thrust of movement, even more resonant.[8]

For the design of this new edition, I referred to the second edition (Christian Bourgois, 1980), which the author had carefully checked over. I have introduced only a slight change by publishing in order the prefaces to the two editions, except for a couple of lines from the first, which were not applicable here. I have corrected a few typographical errors that escaped the author in 1980 and I have put between brackets in the body of the text a few details that in my opinion are needed for today's readers. With the same intentions in mind, I have completed a few references in the notes and added some new ones, each with my initials in order to avoid all confusion.

With the exception of the Preface and the Conclusion (chapter 10), the chapters of this volume had first appeared in the form of isolated articles. In order to publish them as a book in 1974, the author revised and emended them. Here is where they first appeared:

Chapter 1: "Les révolutions du croyable," *Esprit* (February 1969): 190–202; chapter 2: "L'imaginaire de la ville, fiction ou vérité du bonheur?" *Recherches et débats*, no. 69, titled *Oui au bonheur* (1970): 67–76; chapter 3: "Le langage de la violence," *Le Monde diplomatique*, no. 226 (January 1973): 16; chapter 4: "L'université devant la culture de masse," *Projet*, no. 47 (July–August 1970): 843–55; chapter 5: "La culture et l'enseignement," *Projet*, no. 67 (July–August 1972): 831–44; chapter 6: "Minorités," *Sav Breizh. Cahiers du combat breton* (Quimper), no. 9 (July–August 1972): 31–41; chapter 7: "Savoir et société. Une 'inquiétude nouvelle' de Marcuse à mai 1968," *Esprit* (October 1968), special issue titled *Le partage du savoir*: 292–312; chapter 8: "La culture dans la société," *Analyse et prévision*, special issue titled *Prospective du développement culturel* (October 1973): 180–200; this text constituted the "introductory report" prepared for the European Colloquium,

"Prospective du développement culturel" (Arc-et-Senans, April 1972), for which Michel de Certeau was the principal moderator; chapter 9: "Quelques problèmes méthodologiques," *Analyse et Prévision* (October 1973): 13–30; this latter text was the inaugural lecture of the colloquium at Arc-et-Senans.

Part I

Exoticisms and
Ruptures of Language

Chapter 1
The Revolution of the "Believable"

Against Unconsciousness

In the broadest sense of the term, the authorities signify a reality that is difficult to determine, but nonetheless necessary: the air that allows a society to breathe.[1] They allow for social communication and creativity because they furnish, on the one hand, common *references* and, on the other, *possible* paths of pursuit. This is an approximate definition that will have to be more closely defined.

They become corrupted too, but it is by smothering that we realize that they are vitiated. The sickness of confidence, the doubt in respect to political apparatuses and representations (whether monetary or unionized), and the successive forms of a lingering discontent now recall for us this element that is forgotten in times of certainty and that appears indispensable only when it is lacking or rotting away. But must we conclude that, without air, everything would be for the best, that, without authorities, society would be free from all this discontent? It would be tantamount to attending to the death of the patient instead of curing his or her illness.

I share the conviction of those who credit authority with one of the essential problems felt in our increasingly polluted social atmosphere. Many observers make the diagnosis that we live in an air without oxygen, in a vitiated atmosphere. Many also know that talking about it will no longer suffice. The months to come will require hard choices. I believe that the time is coming when fundamental options will have to be made manifest through actions and that they will appeal to our responsibility to make them. This requirement can be measured by the discredit that infects our official "frames of reference" and that attests to a mutation of the "believable."

3

From this point of view, the frames of reference would be proof of a scandalous superficiality on the part of those who wish to collapse a system of authority without preparing its replacement; those who would joyfully throw themselves into violence without accounting for the repression or the fascism that their action would serve; those who would take joy in the perspective of taking part in the great upheaval without wondering what the cost of the spectacle will be and who will pay for it—always the same ones, the minority, those least favored. I find this jubilation disgusting: a lack of consciousness on the part of intellectuals, an art of voyeurs, an "eschatological strike." Even if anger and utopianism are the consequence of a logic and, often, the signs of an absolutely fundamental expression of contestation—I will be blunt—we do not have the right to let ourselves be dragged into it: out of a political sense, out of concern for not substituting the terrorism of an "elite" for a shared responsibility, out of respect for the commitments and spiritual options that are necessarily linked to the risk of living together in a society.

But for the same reason, and because the choices today must be declared in the name of personal political stances, my expression of solidarity is with those who want to "make truth" and grasp in its democratic foundations a social organization of authority. They have the courage to see and to say what they see; they justly refuse to mistake mountains for molehills (to mistake for "authorities" the powers and traditions that merely *use* what they are supposed to *represent*); they are opposed to the demeaning therapeutics that anesthetize a society, that are in collusion with an irresponsibility in order to profit from it, and that exploit a discontent for immediate gain, whose broader implications and consequences are only too predictable.

Between two forms of unconsciousness—one that refuses to see the damages and one that avoids the responsibility of reconstruction, one that denies the problem and one that refuses to seek any solution—we must look closely at the issues of lucidity and action. There is a relation between the discredit that must be challenged and the work that needs to be taken up. To envision once again these two moments affronting one another would be equivalent to better discerning, in the authorities, the latent and mobile condition of every social organization. If, as I believe, they will allow each to articulate its relation with others through its relation with a form of truth, they will represent what has never been acquired and without which our lives would be impossible: a credibility.

The Unbelievable

"It is difficult to believe in something." We heard a young Yugoslav Communist woman say this on television yesterday. She was ready to defend her country against the Soviet Union, even though she had believed in the great homeland of socialism. She felt that close ties with the neighboring bloc still had to be maintained. But, inside of her, something had fallen into silence. She no longer had either a place or a name that would tell her the *truth* of her needs. For political and strategic reasons, all that remained was a utilitarian alliance.

In many countries, relations of confidence are also being frittered away—violently, or without a peep. "Values" that carried solidarities and an entire system of participation have collapsed. *"Nobody" believes in them anymore.* But who is this collective "nobody"? And how is it produced? It is almost impossible to determine what it is. The phenomenon is visible only when it has happened. From its slow preparation only a posteriori symptoms exist. They become evidence when "it's done," when the result is obvious, just as one remembers a dead friend's past, which is suddenly marked with omens that had until then had been imperceptible. In the same way, today, traditions are being challenged; patriotisms are demystified; rules and rites are dismantled; "elders" are discredited ... if at least we believe in the news coming from Africa, America, and Europe, and, no less, in what we have seen. So what has happened that caused *it* to happen? Must it be said that this strange disaffection is furrowing all the lands within the perimeters of "Western" civilization, that there needs to be found, along with the localizations of the malaise, the map of its empire, which is also being dismantled? Quite possibly. But right now no one would dare to take up questions of this order.

Whatever its modalities or its extension elsewhere might be, the discrediting of the authorities constitutes our experience. The symptoms are multiplying. They do not allow us to be rid of the problem by cordoning it off in a given religious, political, or social sector. Resurgent everywhere, they affect all "values" — those of the regime, those of the nation, those of the churches, or those of the stock market. A devaluation is rampant. Right where it is compensated for and hidden, it reappears in a different form. Dogmas, knowledges, programs, and philosophies are losing their credibility; they are shadowless bodies that neither the hand nor the mind can grasp, but whose evanescence irritates or deceives the gesture that continues to seek them;

they merely leave us, tenaciously, with the illusion of the desire to "hold them."

For, among the very ones who state and repeat that we must "stick to" the truths or the institutions of the past, this drive avows the contrary of what it believes it affirms. It displaces the question. It is based on a *need* where a *reality* would have to correspond to this need. An order is indispensable, they declare; the respect for "values" is necessary for the proper functioning of a party, a church, or a university; confidence conditions prosperity. No doubt. Nonetheless, the conviction is lacking. To act *as if* it already existed and because it is a source of national or individual profit is to replace veracity with *utility*. It is to suppose a conviction for the sole reason that a conviction is needed, to decide on a legitimacy because it preserves a power, to impose or feign confidence because of its profitability, to claim belief in the name of institutions whose survival becomes the first object of a politics. A strange inversion! We are glued to expressions and no longer to what is being expressed, to the benefits of an affiliation more than to its reality. The defense of "values," by privileging the service that they render to a group, no longer believes in what the expressions were stating; it believes them lost as soon as it can merely justify them on the basis of a profit margin. Under their breath, how many "realists" or "conservatives" thus acknowledge the devaluation they so loudly fight against!

Others are probably right: "children" no longer admit a spectacle imposed on them in the name of utility and, before the parade of authorities, they dare to cry out that the emperors have no clothes. This game becomes impossible for them, and so they state crudely the interests it masks.

Many wise souls would respond that these things ought to be kept silent, even if they are true. And surely, they thus defend something indispensable to every society: an order, reasons to live in common. But in order to maintain social protests, they happen to challenge the verification whose task it is up to the authorities to objectify to be "received," that is, in order to play their role; they forget that this order has legitimacy only in the name of the affiliations and the participations that it organizes.

I prefer lucidity — perhaps a cruel lucidity — that seeks respectable authorities by beginning with an examination of real situations. Illusion will not lead to truth. Thus we have to confirm what is, the phenomenon that is spreading, whose description alone is not enough, but that first of all must be observed: a growing number of militants are seeking a cause worthy of their generosity without betraying it, but they will not find it. These are exiles from a requirement that no longer has any social representations, but who will only accept a land and credible references.

Emigration

These militants without a cause belong perhaps to a generation of part-timers, deprived of their former lands and capable only of adjoining to the boredom of a job (that has become its own raison d'être) the dreams of grandeur of earlier times. A general complicity seems to drive them since official ceremonies and television favor the same burials. We have too many commemorations and not enough of the present. The country celebrates the grandeur and the celebrities that used to be rallying points, but that are no more, and that are merely needed to reassure, to distract, or to adjoin to everyday prose the relics of antiquated panache. We are no longer done with celebrating the dead. Why should we be surprised by the birth of a need for other festivals? The nation is crammed with commemorative objects, endlessly taken out of their crypts and their scabbards. This accumulation of memories speaks of values belonging only to the past, as if the enormous expansion of a society, like these still-luxuriant trees whose core is rotten, could only justify itself with an inert inner body: the tomb of yesterday. The concern for "the mind, the spirit" goes to the aid of old stones in peril and crowns war veterans.

In truth, the most characteristic feature is of another order. Today, institutions are made more with emigrants than with part-timers; travelers are more numerous than harbingers of nostalgia. The prophet Ezekiel, who was an able poet of the language of imagination, at this juncture furnishes us with a "vision" that now acquires a different — but always formidable — meaning. He lived at a time when Jerusalem, crushed by the Babylonians, was under the yoke of deportations, and when the citizens who were spared believed themselves part of the elite because they remained inside the sacred walls. The prophet saw the chariot with its four cherubim carrying the "glory" of Jehovah fly over the Temple and leave the city (Ezekiel 10–11). The Spirit left the walled confines. The architecture of institutions was being emptied of meaning, and those who were occupying it were only "holding onto" stones, a ground, and brick walls — a foolish possession of the mind. For Ezekiel, the invisible sun of his people had left this earth and taken the road to exile.

Today something similar is happening. An exile is in the works. Like monuments whose official curators believe they are keeping the truth by occupying them, many institutions seemed to be abandoned by those who indeed wish to remain faithful to a requirement of conscience, justice, or truth. What emigrates, sometimes explosively and with protest, but most often silently and as water seeps away, is *adhesion*, like that of citizens, the members of a party, a labor union, or a church. The very spirit that animated these representations now abandons them. It has not disappeared, but it is elsewhere; it has left for foreign lands, far from the structures that its departure changes into grieving spectacles or into liturgies of absence. And if so many important personages now assume a vengeful or tearful tone in order to protest before the heavens against a time stripped of virtue, it is not, according to the image of the prophet, that a "spirit" has died; it is merely that it is no longer living with them. It is not missing; rather, *they* are the ones who miss it.

This paradoxical situation is dangerous and unusual. Even if we admit that a cultural, political, and spiritual ferment is very real but in exile, we cannot minimize the nefarious consequences of a gap opened up between a social language and those who refuse to speak it. This schism slowly tears at the fabric of a culture. It is a violent condition that fosters the proliferation of violence: a collective "madness" multiplies people incapable of sustaining what made their powers so credible, and emigrants, also necessary, caught in the trap of refusal. Opposites are mutually developed and enclosed in extreme positions.

This state of fact drives into a corner and unmasks (but isn't this cynicism another mask?) those who are reduced to exploiting administrative foundations for useful goals. It also demoralizes the people who still adhere to institutions through conviction. They feel they are crying in vain in the midst of ruins. Certain individuals succeed in fleeing, not to construct something elsewhere, but through cowardice, leaving on the spot everything they stood for, forgetting their responsibilities, and finding, in solitude, in sickness, in a career, or in the prestige of "missions" to foreign countries (in the words of French youth, and why not?), the alibi whose general malaise aggravates needs. Others stiffen, they feel that the most reasonable objections are diabolical, they thus think they are defending everything by defending themselves. They literally lose all sense of direction.

Inversely, as we all know, there is a psychology of emigrants found in the proliferation and erosion of ideologies lacking communication; in the utopianism that comes with the impossibility of measuring, through tasks to be done within the nation, the weight of social realities; in keeping leaders in place merely because of a heroic past; or in a history frozen in legend (it is sad to say, but "May" of 1968 is becoming another "Douaumont" of 1916).[2] In order to be a fact and a necessity, spiritual emigration is nonetheless the symptom of a greater social malady. A logic of rupture develops its consequence before personal or collective decisions can intervene. A cultural revolution is accelerated through the very censure that wishes to conceal its effects.

The Refusal of Insignificance

If, perhaps, we live in a civilization that is airing itself out, and if we now live in our social language as if in a rationale (or a system) whose reason is not apparent, we cannot delude ourselves into thinking that an absence prevails in the relation of humans with themselves, or even in the loss of fundamental references that organize collective consciousness and personal life. We can deduce, rather, a lack of coordination between these references and the functioning of sociocultural "authorities." The latter go crazy insofar as they *no longer correspond* to the real geography of meaning.

Analogous to the distance that separates the walls of Jerusalem and the Spirit residing in Babylon, this gap first of all takes the form of a retraction and of an elimination. Becoming increasingly opaque, a marginalized life has no escape in our system of representations. Rural areas and cities—and not just labor unions or universities—are populated with silent subjects. And it is not because they lack ideas or criteria! But their convictions are no longer affiliations. One sign among many is that not long ago, in the course of elections in the unions of several firms (but who will provide the relevant statistics?), workers drew lines through the heads on a list as they voted for it, thus decapitating the apparatus in order to bring it back to its base. On these results, the pontiffs see their names blacked out but without knowing who scratched them off and without understanding why.[3] Those who were supposed to represent the union and who had taken proprietary airs about it have become strangers to the workers; they have gone elsewhere. How many pontiffs have been left aside, decapitated in silence, and do not even realize it yet! Their power functions in such a way that they have no inkling of the silent life, of new questions, of immense aspirations whose clamor dissipates and becomes nothing more than an object of fear, precaution, and tactical response.

I know that it is always easy to mobilize the silent majorities and to believe that in their anonymity they are delegates of power. But the question does not entail warning them or directing them back to ready-made causes. Their invisibility merely corresponds to the rigidity of so many timeworn facades. Behind this political decorum or these liturgies of repetition operates, nonetheless, an immense inner labor that, through a shortsighted policy, too many powers do the best they can to deter from public discussion and take pride in no longer hearing. Abstention, the result of a marginalization of all this labor, instead makes manifest, on the part of the rural population, workers, and youth, a refusal of insignificance.

This refusal normally takes more violent forms. We need only listen to it in order to be persuaded. Violence is first born of a rebellion against institutions and representations that are "beyond belief." It challenges what is meaningless, it says *no* to stupidity, it defends "another country" deprived of signs and of rights—this foreign country that conscience requires and in which are sought common reasons for living. Before mapping out theories on violence, before making an apologia for its cause, as if it were a value and not a goal in itself (I will never do so, for that would surely be a discourse of the same degree of stupidity), we have to recognize it as a fact bearing consequence. In a conflict, it is onething to see what can't be jettisoned from human experience. In the current increase of violence, a claim as essential as that of refusing it would mean losing the right and the taste for life (some things are worth more than life); it is another thing to make a law out of violence—a contradictory position that would forget why we fight, that would remove all meaning from the struggle by depriving it of truly political objectives, that would refuse revolutionary renewal sought by risks taken in common, and that would belittle the will to become a collectivity of human beings as nothing more than the bestial (or natural) "law" of a *struggle for life*.

The violence that is exploding everywhere along the edges of authoritarian regimes is first of all not the stupid savagery that propaganda is claiming it to be. Emerging from social categories from which all responsibility has been carefully retracted before treating them as "irresponsible," it challenges, stirs up, tears to shreds the system that eliminates deeper movements and renewals vital to a country or a group. It tends to inaugurate a reasonable language among people. Behind anger, even if it is unaware of its real name, there is the desire to create a polis and a politics; there is a desire to organize the conditions of life in relation to reasons to live.

Hidden Revolutions

The plan that a group sketches out is no sooner betrayed by a constellation of references. They can exist only for it, and not be recognized beyond these limits. They are nonetheless real and indispensable if communication is to take place. In the depths of the Bolivian mountains (the *Journal d'un guérillero* reported yesterday), as in the suburbs of our cities and in the student assemblies, new paths are being charted.[4] Beliefs are emerging that make a common design *possible*. Once it is spoken—once it can be breathed and felt—a language implies points of references, sources, a history, an iconography, in short, a construction of "authorities." The gesture that demystifies powers and ideologies creates heroes, prophets, and myths. A contradiction? Hardly. For every constructive desire (and every group assumes one), signs of recognition and tacit agreements about the conditions of possibility—if a practicable space is going to be opened—need to be made. Points of reference organize initiatives. A map allows trips to be made. *Inherited* representations inaugurate a new credibility at the same time that they express it.

These nascent credibilities attest to what is most fragile, but also most moving and fundamental, in all social life. They express inventions. But these inaugurations or novelties often move about in the breadth of human history and are noticed only in what is known to be believable and in what is no longer so. That is how, in all modesty, popular language speaks. It is essential that it never state directly but through what it does not deny or what it "inherits." It declares its disagreements only in classifying in different ways whatever carries authority, in such a way that it makes manifest that ineffable *sans quoi* life could not be led. Conviction is shown only through the distribution of what it respects and what it no longer respects; it is expressed by discreetly shuffling the official cards, and through representations that *it does not disavow,* in the way that slang says "you don't make me sick" when it means "I love you."

Any reflection on society has to go back to these beginnings, but with attention drawn to surprises. For travels, ethnology, or meetings with psychoanalysts teach us that *revolutions of the believable* are not always declared. More often, they are more modest in form and thus more formidable, such as inner movements; they produce displacement within affiliation; they surreptitiously reorganize received authorities; in a constellation of references, they happen to favor certain ones and extinguish others—a secret labor that public representations cannot fail to recognize without becoming a meaningless facade.

Inversely, as shown by the "workers' liberation" or "consciousness-raising" movements that associate the power of expression that a group acquires as it is born with individuals who suddenly come to grips with themselves, a life that is closed upon itself needs doors and windows: authorities that can be heard, points of reference that allow a sociocultural "exchange." Some credible signs are needed because they are also an *outlet* of experience, that is, the condition of its possibility.

Words and Representatives

Two life histories indicate the two ways in which the linkage of the tacit geography of experience and visible, existing paths of recourse operates. The former opens a space of words; the latter maps out a topology of action. What becomes a sign of authority in a society takes the shapes of these two figures: discourses (works and texts) or persons (who are also representatives).

Manuel, a vagabond peasant in the slums of Mexico City, was already designating a cultural revolution when, thinking he was a piece of shit, he barely dared (but wasn't it "laughable") ... he dreamed to "find the appropriate words" to "sing the poetry of life," to "express the lowest passions in the most beautiful way".... "win the fight against [him]self." "Men who can write of these things make the world more habitable."[5] A few poetic words, and *perhaps* the world as it is lived begins to change: days are created. Who, within oneself, does not have the experience of what these authorities are opening up? For Manuel, a new space ("a habitable world") would be constituted by these *poetic* "words" built over a "*combat.*" An admirable definition of what true authorities, by shifting things from grounds impossible to grounds possible, can make credible or believable. Daily life, like politics or philosophy, knows these authorities who offer new fields to thought and collective existence.

Elsewhere, these are not common names that become, literally, poetic; rather, these are proper, living names. Thus, lately, an old, hobbled workingwoman, who was really our neighbor in Paris, had a friend drive her to the Père-Lachaise Cemetery. She ambled to the tombs of Edith Piaf and Maurice Thorez. "Now, my friend, don't you see that Edith Piaf, well, she changed everything I believe in. And Thorez, well, he fought for me."[6] These *inherited* authorities say something else than the passive popularity that authoritarian powers use for their propaganda or for their illusions of justification. A similar "gratitude" bears witness to a conviction and its modesty; it is also a judgment. A silent connivance inhabits the depths of an experience that one person expresses and that others declare to be true.

This same story begins over and over again. It can be political or cultural, the two aspects being harder and harder to distinguish from one another. And too often, beneath hierarchies transformed into proprietary rights of what they ought to "permit" and allow to speak, there are obscure struggles against stupidity, collective poetics that nascent authorities arouse and express. This organizing murmur of a real language always surprises the gods in power and the characters on the stages of officialdom when, by chance, they are suddenly silenced.

Every authority is based on an affiliation. Proudhon even says that it is a "matter of faith" and that its basis lies in a "belief."[7] Ultimately, only a spiritual accord provides the exercise of power with legitimacy. It is a conviction (that is a *control*) proportioned to a representation (that is an *issue*). This coordination creates an unowned place constituted through an exchange or a sharing; it "guarantees" communication through a modest and necessary credibility. After all, perhaps language is only the still neutral, but already open, space of a communicability. In any event, the conditions of possibility of an exchange of this kind always remain to be revised or verified, through a sort of cultural revolution that does not forcibly take spectacular forms, but that brings about (if, in a moment of blindness, it is refused) stiffening wherever established authorities reign and emigrations wherever where slow or sudden movements are taking place.

To be sure, every general form of expression in this matter is not only subject to discussion but, in certain respects, both erroneous and ridiculous. Each one positively affirms what is only a negative rule forever indirectly perceived, a condition of possibility that is constantly *lost* from view. Or else, being "obvious," it can also disappear in the remote and ineffable areas of communication. Or else, too, absent, it bears the figure of abstraction and of utopia. But are we grasping the essential other than through what is ridiculous to *state* about it, as if, indeed, without this *sans quoi* nothing could be stated? Social life and the role that authorities play within it thus send us back to what makes them possible.

An "Infinite Task"

A society ultimately results from the response that everyone brings to the question of their relation to a truth and of their relation with others. A truth without a society is merely a lure. A society without a truth is merely a tyranny. So too the double relation — with others and with a truth — calibrates the "philosophical" weight shouldered by the labor of society. In a capital piece of writing, Husserl called this reconciliation an "infinite task." It appeared with the "idea," which in his mind is of Greek origin, of creating a "philosophical community" through a ceaseless "movement of cultural education."[8] This "power of creating cultures" remains, in the language of Husserl, the ambition that humans assigned themselves at a moment of their history, that they claimed to be a sign of their dignity, and that now, at least in Europe, risks putting them in a state of "lassitude," as if they were tired of themselves. But every action, insofar as it is political, is also "philosophical"; every action responds to the task of basing a society on reasons for living that belong both to *all* and to *each*.[9]

For this labor, there is a need, among other things, to reconstitute in common language, and through a critique of traditional stereotypes and powers that have become unthinkable, circuits that make a reciprocal recognition *possible*. Some common points must foster this circulation and mark off its paths. Thus a network of authorities is organized that are at once produced and received. They assure communication. But in that very way, they designate what no one can be identified with, nor be subtracted from, without rejecting the necessary link between the relation with a *truth* and the relation with *others*.

Today attention is drawn toward popular movements that attempt to inaugurate or to restore a network of social relations necessary for the existence of a community, and that react "against the loss of the most fundamental right, the right of a social group to formulate its own *frames of reference* and its own models of conduct."[10] To be sure, in these "references," in their representations, and in the authorities that signify them, there is beneficial inertia in that it forbids to individuals the delusion of self-identity and deters them from private ambitions that would exceed the social body.

However, these references are no less dependent on unstable and successive balances. They change with combined networks (political, economic, cultural) with which they are indelibly associated. Thus, with jurisprudence, laws, constitutions, and the thousand and one forms of a "Law" that remains customary, they move and shift, their aura flickers as criteria of collective consciousness (religious, national, aesthetic, scientific, etc.) appear or disappear. Secret porosities modify the contracts of language, that is, the agreements—that are so difficult to calculate—between the front (that is visible) and the back (that is opaque) of credibility, between what authorities *articulate* and what is *understood* by them, between the communiction they allow and the legitimacy they presuppose, between what they make possible and what makes them credible.

Chapter 2
The Imaginary of the City

The language of the imaginary is multiplying. It circulates everywhere in our cities. It speaks to the crowds, and the crowds speak it too. It is our language, it is the artificial air we breathe, it is the urban element in which we have to think.

Mythologies are proliferating. The fact is clear. It might seem strange at a time when corporate enterprises are rationalized, when sciences are formalized, and when, not without difficulty, society reaches a new state of technical organization. In reality, for reasons that would be too lengthy to analyze, the technical development that inspires the discrediting of ideologies does not efface the needs to which they responded. It turns beliefs into legends that are still laden with meaning (but which? We no longer know). It marginalizes the doctrines that, turned into clouds of sparks, always evoke reasons for being alive.

Every society as a whole learns that happiness cannot be equated with development. It avows the fact by according a growing place to leisure—this nirvana and this "reward" for work—by cultivating the dream of vacations or retirement. Society takes note of it, sometimes with panic, when it sees arising before its eyes the various kinds of disgust and anger of a youth that denounces the common fiction, attests to a general insecurity, and rejects the official discourses whose soft seduction or superb stiffness merely dissimulates their role of papering over misery or plugging holes.

Yet, the imaginary discourse that circulates in the city endlessly speaks of happiness. It inspires us to wonder: exile or creativity, alibi or a work of invention? What, then, are the current forms that inform us about happiness?

Fiction Given to the Eye?

Eros fiction, science fiction...fiction is everywhere. We may take an example as our point of departure. Everywhere we find sexy magazines in our midst. And sex fiction, too. Is the wage earner or white-collar worker who buys one of these magazines when taking the commuter train home seeking an initiation? No, the buyer does not ask from his or her magazine a lesson to be put into practice. On the contrary, he or she reads it precisely *because* a practice will not be engaged. It's sex-fiction: in its images and its "legends" a story about what "is not done," an absent story. Hence a first observation: what goes into that language is what goes out of daily life and what existence no longer offers, either for reasons of fatigue or because one no longer dares think of changing what is possible. Thus, all that can be done is to be satisfied to dream about change. For lack of *doing* something, one *looks on*. As a television commercial puts it, "Take up a sport—in your own armchair!" We are spectators who refuse to be participants.

The imaginary is within the realm of the "visible." It develops a particularly ocular exoticism; because, finally, a logic becomes evident everywhere, even in striptease, when the stripper who bares her body goes hand in hand with the spectator who is dispossessed. What is given to the eye is removed from the hand. The more we *see*, the less we *take*. The boredom of work or the impossibility of acting or doing is compensated for by the surplus of what we see being done. Everything assumes a dream. "Just dream, we'll do the rest," say the Ionel Schein advertisements. The development of the imaginary is the converse of a "civilization" in which visionaries and contemplative souls proliferate. Thus "current events," this visual remainder of action, display the good and bad fortunes of others according to a law that combines the luxury of information with the passivity of its witnesses. Inaction seems to be the price of the image. Amorous pursuits, the bedazzlement of addicts, athletic exploits, or programs of social renewal pour into imaginary literature and offer, along with the spectacles themselves, an alibi of action. We only need to recall Borges's *Chronicles of Bustos Domecq* and his chapter "Esse est percipi," "To exist is to be seen." Is it only the image of reality that remains? Yes, when the act that posits it is exiled from existence.

In any case, insofar as the objects that furnish the imaginary establish the topography of what we can no longer accomplish, we can wonder if, inversely, what *is most seen* does not define what *is most lacking*.

That itself invites us to take the themes of this literature seriously. For example, what are the magazines or photo-novels that form the base really telling? Over and through the sentimental bliss, the ecstasies of love, or bodily relations, they speak of *communication*. But a successful communication that overcomes obstacles and conflicts is not what is encountered in life. It is a legendary territory. It replaces the paradise of beliefs that have generally become unbelievable and that once opened a future of communion among saints. It displaces hopes that have themselves become no less unbelievable, that used to announce, with the days following the momentous evenings, the coming of a classless society. A continuity and relays among "utopias" indicate the trace of a function of the imaginary and a remainder of different kinds of paradise. No matter what, the present figure of the imaginary speaks of an absence in the most positive terms. It has been attesting to what, decades ago, David Riesman called "the lonely crowd," a name he ascribed to the sickness from which modern Western society suffers.

Mythologies say what is being sought "in the image" because no one dares to believe in it anymore, and often what *fiction* alone is able to give. They betray at once hunger and action. They translate at the same time a refusal to lose and a refusal to act. Thus, too many words or images tell of a loss and an impotence, that is, the opposite of what they display. The great programs of a "new society" slyly substitute the message of discourses for action that would change our society. Revolutionary ideologies compensate for the deficit of will or the privation of power. Religion fiction, revolution fiction, eros fiction, or drug fiction insert into fiction the object that they display and, as if in a mirror, they produce but the inverted image of happiness whose flashes of sunshine they multiply in the urban landscape.

Discourse of Advertising

It would thus be vapid to believe that myths disappeared with the advent of rationalization. If we believed that the streets had been disinfected of myth, we would be deluding ourselves. On the contrary, myths reign over them. They spread out on surfaces of images the dreams and the repressed of a society. They surge up on all sides, but through outlets other than those of yesterday.

They invade advertising, whether in the form of "chocodreams," of a "direct return to native soil," of associations between "saving accounts" and "dreams," between "happiness" and "security," or between "celebration" and a bottle of Vichy water... In consumer society, such are the paltry joys of the rich. However, advertising parcels out in pocket money the equivalent of a golden age. Objects unfold a red carpet to a utopia that, far from being absorbed by consumerism, transforms the vocabulary of exchange, that is, commerce, into an imaginary literature, into a "Frigidaire mystique," as Lucien Goldmann so aptly put it. Refrigerators or food processors that fascinate the gaze of those who pass by replace the old words in order to assure, along with the tantalizing object, that "in two minutes we'll be able to celebrate!" Planted in the paradise garden of poster ads, the fruits of happiness are within arm's reach. They bring into proximity the eschatological end. They spell out an immemorial time by fragmenting its dream and by refusing its distance. But in reality, as in the way of words, objects always defer the desires they inspire beyond themselves toward other objects.

These consumer items are the subjects of every sentence. They have as their calling card the smile that modifies them through a sign of expectation and encounter, or the seductive gesture that encompasses the car and the washer with its dance. Thus is formed a discourse. It stipples the subway tunnels with signs of happiness where, squeezed like sardines, five million people circulate at rush hour. But what does it say, if not, with all the consumer goods that flicker on the main subway routes, the end that must halt the crowd's movement?

This imaginary discourse of commerce is pasted over every square inch of public walls. It unfurls from street to street and is scarcely interrupted by the intersection of avenues. The modern city is becoming a labyrinth of images. It is endowed with a graphics of its own, by day and by night, that devises a vocabulary of images on a new space of writing. A landscape of posters and billboards organizes our reality. It is a *mural language* with the repertory of its immediate objects of happiness. It conceals the buildings in which labor is confined; it covers over the closed universe of everyday life; it sets in place artificial forms that follow the paths of labor in order to juxtapose their passageways to the successive moments of pleasure. A city that is a real "imaginary museum" forms the counterpoint of the city at work.

This language of utopia is prolonged only when it moves from billboards to graffiti of protest, or from the underground tunnels of the subway to the corridors of the university; when it makes a sharp turn from solicitation to protestation. An identical mural writing announces that ready-made happiness is for sale. From the billboard to graffiti, the relation of offer and demand is inverted: but, in both cases, representation is "manifest" because it is not given. In this respect, refusal speaks the same language as seduction. Here too, commercial discourse continues to tie desire to reality without ever marrying the one to the other. It exposes communication without being able to sustain it.

This counterpoint of mural language has, moreover, many other equivalents. The dream irrupts in the fissures of the workweek, on weekends, and in leisure time. It emerges in the "vacation" of time with the artifices of the countryside or the freedoms of the "party." But it also ends up on the psychoanalyst's couch, where the client reclines, a spectator of the dreams he or she recounts and the object of a faceless concentration behind his or her back. The imaginary haunts sensitivity groups, organizing legends of a press that manufactures "good" and "bad," both "idols" and "resistance groups." It inhabits a common vocabulary and originates from everywhere. It is invested in technical organizations and, perhaps, turns them into dream factories. It is the indefinite water that laps the shores of scattered islets of reason, sites that new enterprises seek to capture and to exploit.

The Body of Happiness

It has often been noted that the universal infiltration of the imaginary was characterized by a growing eroticization. Eroticism immediately follows food products and comes before everything else (happiness, health, etc.) in a classification of the types of solicitation in order of importance. It is the normal end point of publicity that celebrates the sensations of eating and drinking, the marvels of the mouth and lips, the ease of unhindered movement, the joys of the flesh, the nasal metamorphoses of breathing, or the liberations of the body that loses weight and gravity. Announced everywhere, along with a celebration of the senses, is a celebration of the body. But it is a fragmented body, categorized by virtue of an analytical dissection, cut into successive sites of eroticization. The dispersion of pleasures replaces former unities with a sensorial space. A metaphor of happiness, the body is serialized. It is antireason, but it is structured in the fashion of contemporary reason as its negative and its equivalent.

We have to call into question this "common" language that Freud, when he wrote *Civilization and Its Discontents,* distinguished from cultural or aesthetic "sublimations" reserved for an elite. The "ordinary man" is the fundamental problem. Thus, what is striking in the social discourse of happiness is the alternation between the confessions of the heart and the baring of the body. Love stories and eroticism no doubt tell of the same movement, but on two different registers. For both, however, an unveiling takes place.

It can be interpreted as a sexual or a sentimental exhibitionism. And often rightly so. But this gesture contains a more fundamental meaning. It seeks to *display what is hidden* and, thereby, to withdraw what separates. The confession of the heart and, in a more radical but (paradoxically) more symbolic way, the undressing of the body function as the allegory of a quest for pleasure, for communion, or for reality. It is a demystification even if it still retains the form of a myth. The search for a truth is thus "represented."

From this point of view, three properties characterize the return of the body within the imaginary. It expresses a *transgression,* it connotes a *communication,* and it aims at the grasping of a *reality.*

From the "bodily cares" and the weight-watcher diets all the way up to "the expressiveness of the body" or to the techniques of love, the fantastic dimension of the body translates a *transgression* with respect to societal norms. Is there a more rigorous and more ritualized code than that of clothing? It classifies, it distinguishes, it hierarchizes, it guarantees the secret contracts of the group. It maintains social "distinctions," cultural status, and the distance between classes. This code cannot be broken, nor can social decency be compromised without transgressing an established order. To be sure, this "indecent exposure" will be tolerated as long as it is more or less "theatrical." Thus everyone will take pains to prove that "it's only a representation." But in itself the language of the body is egalitarian. It removes defensive and protective barriers. Although still in the mode of fiction because it only lays blame on signs and clothing, it bares and relativizes securities, patents, and social privileges.

Then again it tells the tale of a *communication* linked to this risk of social transgression. In every society, as Freud showed in various ways, Eros is controlled or repressed by the group it threatens. Thus the first communication, that of bodies in love, is at once an object of desire and an object of fear. With respect to the law, it does not conform. At the very least, it does not suffice for it to conform. Men and women are judged on the basis of their sexual relations, and here they no longer have the assurance of social rank. Eros is an irreducible violence. It restores at once both conflict and pleasure. It shakes to the core all public contracts. Perhaps, by exiling it within the image, people seek to guarantee its presence; but there too the discourse of the body speaks of internal *relations* in the society that returns to it through the detour of the imaginary.

In a word, a kind of ferocity or nostalgia stirs up from within the media-produced mythology of happiness, translating the desire to attain *something short of representations*. Clearly, the baring of the body still remains in the order of representation. But the social "clothing" of representation designates its opposite as bare and barren reality. Inside of language, the naked body is the theme that aims at both the referent and the medium of language. It is the emergence (betrayed by its very inscription on the surface of images) of cultural movement that sets out in quest of "nature," along with the entire range of mythological images of a return to childhood and to the nudity of paradise, to the originary immediacy of nonknowledge, and to "reality" in its perpetually veiled condition. Behind social barriers, beneath the necessary artifices of work, there would be—there is, the images tell us—a tree of life: the body, the concealed and forbidden fruit, the pleasure in sleep, the promise of health, the fountain of happiness. This "deep body," messianic body, and trace of the body-God would remain for the social body its lost and long-awaited truth.

From the Exotic Body to Critical Speech

Laden with meaning, these three traits of the body remain no less the traits of a representation. In a broad sense, they are stuck in a language that always vacillates between display and camouflage because it spends its time in deceptively concealing what it nevertheless unveils. Transgression turns to the profit of the techniques of consumerism that rehabilitate and exploit it. Communication is filtered through forms of social censure. It moves, by being alienated within, into spectacles devoted to the love of others or into the "exercise of pity" that dialogue becomes. Bare reality forever appears only in the form of "possessions"; it is fragmented and hidden in an exchange of pleasures or of consumer goods.

The body situates a new exoticism, our own, by expressing the demystification of the utopias—lunar or ethnological—of former times. The vocabulary of health and of medicine, of eroticism, or of drugs furnishes a site for our legends that are destined, as they have always been, to steal away the black sun they announce.

In a word, as Freud put it, "happiness is not a cultural value."

The sciences of language are probably only one more sign of what representations have *become*. The techniques of suspicion, psychoanalytic and sociological alike, depend on the society they analyze. Speech, as well, by becoming critical, avows in its own way what it is denouncing. Already on billboards the name that is adjoined to the object being shown is the ironic evocation of its absence. The argument of the image contradicts it. But by endlessly designating things, words are in a position that differs from theirs. Words name that position precisely because they have nothing to give; they spell out absences by distinguishing realities. Signs of distancing, they postulate dispossession as the very condition of designation. They represent, with respect to every form of happiness, a critical moment.

Speech, I believe, has become a *denaturing* act, an act that culturally posits a distancing with respect to nature. It is also tantamount to admitting the illusion of economic prosperity or of the progress of consciousness. One does not speak with one's mouth full. In order to be pronounced, speech is opposed to eating, and its content says nothing other than just that. It retracts from consumption the meaning it puts forward. Through its function it is destined to become the labor that constantly insinuates the dangerous gap or the critical rift of a lack in the dumb certainty of satisfaction. It denies the reality of pleasure in order to institute symbolic meaning.

Words, nonetheless, are not everything. The inverse is also true. Words are nothing or, rather, an "almost nothing." Like an acid, they eat at (and sculpt?) the immediate *given* of the imaginary. They eat into the shell that encloses happiness; by opening it, they bore holes into it. Surely, whether philosophical, poetic, theological, or born of a popular "wisdom" that is bereft of these comely adjectives, speech, in the magical act of being pronounced, does not make disappear the immense deployment of possessions that are given to be seen. It is itself taken and nourished in the very element out of which it emerges. But the sole fact of speech restores the absence, prohibits identification with the imaginary, and, in the form of a *no*, permits a movement that perhaps is one of meaning.

Having a Blast

From then on, a space of play unfolds between speech and the imaginary. It specifies the enigma of these forms of happiness promised by the image and denied by words. The discourse of images represents them; the syntax of words refers them to a meaning that is lacking. But from this play the tacit rules are indicated on the poster or billboard by the finger pointed toward the spectator or by the indiscreet mention of a price: *it costs money.* Such is the "morality" these languages formulate. They mutually refer to a third element that can be neither stated nor seen: *the gesture.* The allegory of the imaginary and critical speech point in this way to the veritable site of happiness, a site that cannot be placed in the space of the image or in the coherence of the phrase: *the act of spending.*

This "act" restores the moments that escape the spatial continuities of discourses. It is, like time itself, what exists only when it is being lost. In all likelihood it will assume different forms, going as far as the political or ceremonious gesture of *being* spent, or as far as the revolutionary act of preferring a founding moment to a heritage, or as far as the "madness" of receiving the grace of happiness in the loss of profits, even the profit "gained" through consciousness of the act. But this happiness is already figured in the mythology that represents transgression, risky communication, or a meaning to be unveiled. Finally, reality that is unveiled is not hidden in a "nature" that can be situated somewhere. It can be identified with something undefined: with action itself.

Perhaps, after all, imaginary literature in its totality signifies nothing other than this irreducible surplus with respect to any margin of social profit, a luxury that cannot be eliminated from the most rational of all societies. In the flickering of its consumable fictions, the imaginary would bear the truth it could never offer. A metaphor of history, it transposes into an act of *seeing* what can only be found in the act of *doing.* It calls thus for the denegation of speech, and yet it is also incapable of replacing the praxis that alone provides meaning.

In an elementary way, it could be said that our age of mass media transmutes society into a "public" (a key word that replaces the substantive "people"), that it pigeonholes happiness in the icons of objects offered for consumption, and that it mobilizes the verb in the direction of denegation ("please be hidden, object!"). It combines the epiphany of the king-object and suspicion with regard to all represented forms. It similarly coordinates the language of figuration and the language of lack. The relation of these two idioms posits the ambiguity of happiness. It might already be uttering reality, but without being able to say *where* that reality is found.

It would be impossible to conclude that happiness is subject to an indefinite postponement of something that is forever to come, toward a hereafter that is always renewable and that would merely indicate the vanity of its pursuit and the insignificance of its end. On the contrary, I believe this movement finds its support and jurisdiction in the act to which the combination of the two languages and their impossibility of enclosing it in a discourse refer: *to have a blast*. This "luxury" of celebration is that without which there is no more human experience, the "madness" without which there is no reason. It may simply consist, at least for the humble wage earner in Rio, in spending half of one's annual salary during Carnival. For the lover, it might mean "tossing out the window" all one's savings in order to offer a gift. For the person on vacation, it might mean "blowing a wad." A strange and sacred generosity.

To be sure, a society controls the outlets when it can no longer make this same gesture and when it prefers the position of the spectator to that of the actor. Thus a Malthusianism of risk and of happiness (the two go together) puts off till vacation the celebration that is eliminated from political life for reasons of economic profit or national security. At that moment celebration is marginalized. It is often now limited to the cultural sectors; and yet they are themselves objects of jealousy as much as they are condemned by the moralists of economic or sexual "production" — ascetics who are, moreover, hypocrites, for their unremitting work is a game of the privileged class that cannot be avowed in public.

Despite all else, there remains the link between the happiness of living and the danger of existing, between *finding* and *losing*. It even inverts the techniques of assurance or the signs of prosperity in ways of venturing forth: medicine is metamorphosed into drugs; cars, into risks.

This redeployment from goods owned to goods to be lost probably gives its truest measure to the economy that links production to consumption. To consume also means to annihilate and to lose. There, surely, is the economy that articulates its end and jurisdiction by merely stating "Spend!" There is the economy that rejects its own law and retracts into a capitalistic stinginess by declaring, "Just get rich!" To this rift between *spending* and *saving* correspond many great political and cultural options. At the grand outer limit, it is the option of the revolutionary nation that prefers to run the risk of living over attaining goods, or even that of conservative groups that the fear of risking their heritage destines to fetishize the happiness that they are precisely in the process of losing.

This collective or individual "ethic" might be seen as paradoxical. Yet it must be reiterated. Whoever wants to *conserve* is established in the *dependency* of an order, a possession, or a science, and subject to the law (of profit or of assurance) that eliminates through risk the happiness that it promises. It alienates itself. It no longer "holds" onto happiness but onto representations. For there seems to be happiness only where the *other* is the condition of *being,* where people can *have a blast,* where the conservation of goods is distorted through an expenditure made in the name of others, of an elsewhere or of the Other, where the celebration of a communal generosity, a scientific adventure, a political foundation, or an act of faith intervenes.[1]

Chapter 3
The Language of Violence

When the American B-52s carpet-bomb North Vietnam, or when the Chilean military police beat and massacre the nation's citizens, it is silly to *talk about* violence. Powers in control turn declarations of peace, justice, liberty, or equality into a language of derision. The powers multiply them by multiplying violence. How can these words be repeated after declarations that are devoid of content? The discourses of good conscience pick up the trash left in the wake of power, and they make it pass for truths. In fact, the hypocritical phraseology or the ostentation of great principles can no longer even mask its impotence. This derisory "nobility" only claims to preserve a decor of "values." It is no longer of interest to us.

But we have to take control of this humiliated language, we have to see it as the symptom of a general condition. Such as it is, fallen, it displays what Western societies have done with it, and I cannot exempt myself from this common situation by flashing my intellectual union card. Violence is not in the first place a matter for reflection, nor is it an object that can be put before the eyes of an observer. It is inscribed in the place from which I speak of it. Violence defines that place. What must be taken into account before any examination of the facts is that violence is branded on this "sick language" (J. L. Austin) that is objectively servile and utilized—no matter what he says—by the system it challenges, and is taken, carried off, "refashioned" by the commercial networks whose socioeconomic function bears meaning heavier than all ideological contents. A text is transformed into a commodity and into a symptom of the system that moves and sells it. What it tells changes nothing. The prerequisite to a discussion on violence, therefore, becomes what is betrayed by this rigged and pathetic discourse.

If, by violence, we mean a growing distortion between what a discourse says and what a society does with it, then this very discourse functions as a manifestation of violence. It becomes itself a language of violence. But the return of violence in language not only indicates to us a new status of discourse in society and the demystification of power with which it has been accredited since the Enlightenment; by analyzing how the insignificance of what is *said* is produced, we also obtain a means of discovering what has to be *done*.

A Literature of Desertion

Two centuries of linguistic analysis have shown that language does not make manifest the presence of things, no longer yields presences, and no longer produces a world of transparence. Rather, it is an organized place that allows things to happen. It does not give what it says: it lacks being. Thus it can be dealt with. Defection of being has as a corollary the operation whose space and object are furnished by language. Perhaps that is why a division characterizes contemporary culture. In scientific fields, an artificial and decided language articulates practices. In its literary trappings, language is destined to tell stories. It becomes a novel. Rather than epiloguing on the causes and the stages of this situation, we would do well to recall a massive effect of literary production. Increasingly, this language-fiction is the mask and instrument of violence.

Political discourse does not state the ulterior motives that produce its effects. But it does serve those motives. Ideologies rehearse truths that can no longer be believed, but ideologies are always distributed by the institutions that stand to profit from them. Advertising spells out the paradises that a productivist technocracy organizes offstage. Mass media internationalize anonymous broadcasts, aimed at everyone and true of no one, according to the law of a market of signifiers that furnishes an indefinite margin of profit to its directors. The market can only hope to produce oblivion among its consumers.

Hegel diagnosed a similar situation in eighteenth-century culture. The content of discourse of that time, he said, was "the perversion of every concept and every reality," that is, "the universal deception of oneself and of others."[1] Today the phenomenon is different: there no longer exists any truth at stake in the game of deceit. The possibility of deceiving has vanished. *Who* is deceiving *whom*? To give an example of this fact: spectators are not the dupes of the media theater, but they refuse to say so. Their activity is concentrated in the labor that is required for the purchase of a television set; before the images that multiply the prestige-commodity, they can be passive and think no more about it.[2] They abstain. The organizers of the "theater" thus fail to grasp those before whom they display the signifiers aimed at engendering needs. But the organizers are also absent from their products. They obey the laws of a market. The senders and the receivers are equally lacking in this language that develops its own logic in between. A neutrality occupies the space in which, formerly, positions were inverted and cleverly deceived each other. A literature of perversion follows a literature of defection.

The language-commodity does not state either its use or what determines that use. It is the effect, the product of a violent system that, when grasped in its cultural form, disarticulates speech and language, constraining the former to be silent and the latter to proliferate indefinitely.

What issue might be found in culture itself? "Escape into silence" (C. B. McPherson)? A return to rarefied spaces is elsewhere the fact of communities, in which a practice of physical encounter takes up words at their beginnings and initiates, with precaution, an aphasic therapy caused by an overproduction of signifiers. For its part, literary practice deconstructs their syntax and vocabulary in order to make them avow what they repress. It also seeks an oneiric use of words; it cultivates the lapses and the interstices, and everything that, by making clear "the impoverishment of speech" (Artaud), cuts across and through linguistic systems. However, these violences enacted upon language designate its function, but they do not change it. They participate in what they are denouncing. In exiting from insignificance, they remain impotent.

Power without Authority: Bureaucratic Tyranny

This literature of defection is in fact nothing more than the corollary of a power without authority. To be sure, political tradition has long realized that "every state is grounded on force," and that the state assumes domination. But tradition affirms that state is established only in exercising a *legitimate* power. As Passerin d'Entrèves has shown, at stake is an "institutionalized" or "qualified" force.[3] This legitimacy does not originate in regulatory or ordering procedures, but from the authority that is recognized in them and that combines with individual "abnegation" (Freudian *Versagung*) of the capacities offered through the organization of a group.[4] What legitimate power *proscribes* is based on what it *allows* (or makes possible) to be done or thought.

In fact, until now it compensated for what it forbade to *do* through what it allowed to *believe*. It could aim at the credibility of a god, of a man, or of a social category—in other words, an *other*—in order to balance the resistance of individuals or groups to the prohibitions imposed on them. It played on this authority tied to a visible delimitation of the other in order to obtain abnegation and recognition in the remaining local pockets of public life. But, in being constituted as a pedagogical state, it did not cease to extend the public domain and thwart its relation with a particular power. In principle, the state-school imposes itself on all and belongs to none. It suppresses its own limit. It destroys what grounds at once an authority, a control, and a struggle: the relation with an other. Its objective language is given as a law without borders, like that of the market and that of history. Bearing a gray and stone-wall demeanor, leaders conceal their violence in a universal and requisite system. The particular group of producers erases its mark in the expansionist logic of its products. If it is true that every order upholds a necessary relation with the violence of an irreducible other (signified in a mythic crime, in a public conflict, in a social category), we have in this instance the perfect crime, one that leaves in language only the trace of its anonymity.[5]

Thus is developed a power without authority because it refuses to express itself, because it is without a proper name, without anyone explicitly authorizing it or who might be held accountable for it. It is the "rule of anonymity," a "tyranny without a tyrant," in other words, the bureaucratic regime. This system of universal alienation replaces responsible leaders and directors with profiteers. Subjects are replaced by those who are exploited. Opaque to itself, it takes endless advantage of its indistinction, and thus loses more and more of its credibility.

To survive means, then, to flee or to shatter the anonymity of which language is but the symptom; it is to restore the struggle on which order is formulated. "The more public life tends to bureaucratize, the greater the temptation to have recourse to violence."[6] More broadly, for lack of being "allowed" through the recognition of irreducibly different forces, the capacity for action flows back in the direction of civil disobedience. It reintroduces the violence of the other.

This totalitarian regime probably inherited its model from science. It is essential that the discourse that organizes its practices be held by "anybody" but by no one in particular. In reality, the neutrality of scientific discourse, combined with the obfuscation of its function, with the disappearance of an acting organization, with the obliteration of the social places in which it is constructed, has turned it into the discourse of unconscious servility. Today it works in the service of military development that mobilizes the essential labor of all research, fixes its objectives, and is the beneficiary of its own acceleration.[7] A violent power is surreptitiously introduced in the empty place occupied by "anybody." But if it furnishes a hidden director for the expansion of operative science, he is determined by its logic; he is marked by a bellicose role, but all the while remaining unable to control the inner principle of its progress.

A Society of Eviction

The most operative language thus becomes the most impotent. By obstructing its relation with productive forces and responsible subjects, it has turned the violence it claimed to suppress into an anonymous proprietor. It has shaken up the system of eviction, the latter finally affecting subjects themselves (who are constituted as such in desire and in speech only by locating the resistance of the other). People are ultimately evinced by the system whose products reiterate and multiply the law posited with its principle. The anonymous universalism of the city, of culture, of work, or of knowledge develops the impossibility of being situated as different and of reintroducing alterity—hence conflict—into language. An aggressivity is diffused within it from below, but without ever modifying the public law or finding any escape other than the unconscious, literary fiction, or vacations.

It is striking to see how the fear of being *de trop*, as engendered by this system, is generalized. Parents, children, bourgeois, farmers, teachers, men, women...In various ways, the machine threatens to collapse particularities and differences. It excommunicates groups and individuals who are marginalized, forced into defending themselves as exiles, and dedicated to discovering themselves within the repressed.

This system, all the way from science to the mass media, unleashes a monstrous proliferation of intermediary places, a neutral, standardized zone in which is endlessly repeated the form of an abstract universal filled, now and again, by the particulars on which its modulation is based. This anonymous clerical order is slowly taking over the entire social field. It fatigues both senders and receivers, who are crushed by mediation. Along the leading edges in the progress it produces is a multiplication of flight or of rebellion.

Thus *is reproduced* within the system what it produces on the outside. The effect is seen in the assimilation of colonized nations, in the elimination of their alterity, in their being aligned with the law of the market.[8] Those exercising power are not excluded themselves, for they too feel the effect of the law of eviction that was aimed at others. Caught in their own machinery, they are dispossessed of a power they must be content to enjoy in their turn only in irresponsibility, without controlling it, little by little stuck in lassitude or giddiness by their inability to act in ways other than by exchanging, exploiting, and sometimes fleeing the best places.

The Practice of Blasphemy

Acts of violence are correctly designated as "manifestations." They seek to shatter and uncover the alienating economy of the medium and the totalitarianism of identity. In this respect, outrage becomes a "moral passion." It turns into a gesture because an embargo has been placed on words. The trashers who toss bricks at the screens of IBM computers or car windows are doing the same thing as the writer who deconstructs language, but they have no text to work with. The fissure that they mark in the objective network of signifiers is the equivalent of a lapse in language. Their act cries out in protest against a saturated universe. The recurring emphasis on anonymity creates the analogy of an "interference" in which speech initially takes the form of a rupture, a gap, or a blasphemy.

This is probably an extreme case. We can nonetheless predict that it is going to spread throughout Western societies. Certainly the present situation initially develops an escapism: departures toward open spaces suddenly take place, but these are spaces in which the economy of the medium closely follows its travelers, at least when it does not precede them. Will this expansion be compensated for, as A. Moles believes, through the formation of individual "shells" whose carapaces are the protective layers of automobile cells, apartment cells, and autodidactic cells whose hardened exterior will be proportioned to the codified development of constraints and services? Will this universe not be turned into an anthill? For the moment, the facts tend to show that everywhere *aggression* responds to *eviction*.

The defining characteristic of this aggression is a way of treating language, and not the sum of a few more places, functions, or statements. Whether in political, erotic, or gratuitous ways, outrage abuses language. It does not ground it; it cuts it. It is a style, a way of speaking, an ephemeral feast. It surges up like the absurd. In that very way, it reveals violence burrowed within an order. It unleashes fury. It draws the anger out of those who are the pinions in a system of production. But after this game of truth has brought violence back to the surface of an order, what can happen?

More basically, the violent act is the signature of the irruption by a group. It seals the desire to exist of a minority that seeks to consitute itself in a universe in which it is *de trop*, simply because the minority has not yet been able to affirm itself. Birth cannot be dissociated from a violence. Every order, every legal status has an origin marked in blood—even if, once established, it seeks to have this origin forgotten. What would be the most visible nations, where would be the rights of man, of labor unions, or even of paid vacations without the battles that made them possible? What would every language be without the shrieks and the violences on which each of them is built? But we are perhaps in an order that, having succeeded too well in disaffecting social life from the danger of the other, tolerates fewer and fewer births and for this reason makes them all the more difficult and violent.

Struggle, Taking Charge of Violence

Despite all else, this violence inhabits *expressivity*. It remains in a discourse of protest even if it is the underside and the rift of the universal discourse of mediation. It is not freed from the sterility or impotence basic to language disconnected from the violence it denies. In other words, it does not articulate one distinct and avowed force among others. It is a sign. It opens possibilities. In this way, it is pertinent. But it does not create. It defeats, but it does not inaugurate.

It must also be stated that the act of violence situates itself within the order of defiance if it is not inscribed in a work. It is identified with the ostentatious jousting of yesteryear. It bears the mark of an aristocratic privilege. This luxury is basically still granted in a society of spectacle. It irritates it in order to fill it with emotion, but not enough to shake it to its roots, since it retains the means of becoming a stray news item and of thus diffusing the particularity that, momentarily, was torn away from its law. Besides, it is hardly surprising that the intellectual bears a complacency for this artistocratic gesture of violent defiance. It discovers a means of saving — with this underside of language that remains a sign — the place that it had initially claimed to set aside for knowledge.

What is true is that violence indicates a necessary change. Neither the alienating security of an anonymous order nor the defiance of pure violence can respond to the task made urgent under the reigning tautology of commodities with which the salvation of its new serfs seems to be identified. Only a struggle can take charge of what violence takes pleasure in signifying, and of creating a labor built on its forces. The demystification of language through violence opens onto the horizon of political battle, which — in actual, not literary ways — implies taking seriously and risking confrontation with repressions that defend and promote a difference. This probably also attests to the vanity of publishing yet another piece of writing on the topic. At least it means that what Merleau-Ponty once said can be invoked again:

> The taste for violence, [Weber] says, is a hidden weakness; the ostentation of virtuous feelings is a secret violence. . . . [T]here is a *force,* that of the true politician, which is beyond these [prestiges]. . . . Because his action is a "work," a devotedness to a "thing" (*Sache*) which grows outside him, it has a rallying power which is always lacking in undertakings which are done out of vanity.[9]

Part II

New Marginalisms

Chapter 4
Universities versus Popular Culture

Today the university must resolve a problem for which its tradition did not prepare it: the relation between culture and the massive expansion of its "recruitment." The linkage now requires the university to produce popular culture.

Institutions are collapsing under this stupendous burden, and for some reason they are equally unable to respond to the demands of a endless flow of candidates knocking on their doors. The mentality and future of these students are foreign to the current goals of higher education. This double shock has caused the university to be riven into opposite tendencies. Some seek to protect themselves from the tidal wave by fortifying the outer walls of their citadels through the adoption of strict admissions policies, and to toughen the "requirements" of each discipline by exercising greater control. This policy of "we shall never surrender" aims at defending the honor and the rights of established disciplines. Others allow the mass of students to trample the flower beds of tradition, counting on the resulting "mix" and exchange to build a new cultural language. For a long time, because of the uncertainties and the stammerings to which it has often given rise, this policy of dialogue has been reduced to islets perceived as harbors of sloppiness, narrowly defined ideologies, and incompetence. Its "products" are marked off and treated accordingly. In both instances, it is the students who foot the bill; they are the ones destined for the slaughterhouse of the final exam or for unemployment because of a lack of technological training.

Between these two options, between the unusually hard points and the unusually soft crossroads, there exists an entire spectrum of solutions. They enrich experience and multiply confusion. As a whole, the hard line wins among teachers, with the apparent justification afforded them, on the one hand, by hesitant support, insufficient means, and the feeble results of innovation, and, on the other hand, by respect for tradition, an ethics of professional "correctness," and the pressure of political contingency. One of the most moderate professors of the Sorbonne recently stated—correctly—that the law of orientation was being applied today as the Edict of Nantes had been before Louis XIV revoked it: that is, in a way that was increasingly intolerant for the new options that it was officially supposed to "recognize."

Through the manifold experiments of the university in its labors, different problems emerge—even if, simultaneously, their solutions become distant. Demographic, economic, administrative, or political data set aside (essential to the discussion, but sketched out elsewhere), the problems here, insofar as they refer to a capital urgency for the life of the nation at large, will be envisaged as both the *absence* and the *necessity* of popular culture within the university.[1]

From Selection to Production

Aiming to provide a research pedagogy for a relatively restricted population of students before the advent of primary school (about 1900) and secondary school (since 1935), the university of the past produced an "elite culture" in the best sense of the term.[2] The same social meaning did not hold for different faculties. In law, medicine, or pharmacy, cultural selection preferred socioprofessional privileges, but this was not the case for the humanities and the sciences. But, on different registers, culture remained the means by which a strongly hierarchized society maintained a code with clear criteria and assured its own homogeneity on the basis of a relatively stable elite. Culture was thus the result of the principle of rarity.

In a short span of years, from 1960 to the beginning of the school year slated for 1970, student populations tripled. The reasons for the explosion included demographic growth; free secondary school and, consequently, the increased number of high-school graduates; and finally, the increase in the standard of living, which resulted in a greater demand for participation in cultural activities, social promotion, and thus access to higher education. From a total of 215,000 in 1960, the student population expanded to 736,000 a decade later. In addition to this quantitative development, a *qualitative* significance must be recognized. The new sets of problems cannot be solved merely by multiplying faculties and campuses, expanding lecture halls, expanding the base of teaching personnel, or revising an archaic administration incapable of responding to the needs of the greater national enterprise. The massive entry of the middle classes into the university poses an entirely different problem.

The relation of culture to society has been transformed: culture is no longer *reserved* for a given milieu; it no longer belongs to certain professional *specialties* (teachers or liberal professions); nor is it any longer a *stable* entity defined by universally received codes.

René Kaës summed up matters perfectly when, at the end of a study of culture, apropos of workers he noted,

> They look forward to a school that would be a *place to meet and to learn social life*, a microcosm and prefiguration of adult society, and *a site of practical and theoretical preparation for everyday life*, especially that of *work*. . . . The majority of workers attend to what they feel is most urgent: a need to assure mobility and ease in social relations, to get away from indistinction and professional expendability, and an uneasy sense about a professional future.[3]

This anticipation is frustrated, thwarted. Thus one of these laborers happened to define culture as a forbidden fruit, an interdiction, "a treasure surrounded by a crown of thorns." Reports submitted by professional search committees show that within the university culture it is defined by a "taste," by an "inner circle," by a system of references to a type of reasoning, in short, by something *unsaid* that belongs to the group and, by virtue of this fact, is prohibited to others.[4]

In other ways, tens of thousands of students share today the same sentiment. Subjected to intellectual schemes that they find organized neither in relation to their questions nor to their future, they no longer grasp the cultural or social value of *instrumentality* in the instruction "given" to them. Often all that remains is yet another wall to climb, one more obstacle to overcome, one more imposed requirement that they must satisfy in order to gain access to the employment found on the other side. From this standpoint, the university resembles a police force, or else it creates "flunkies" along with the elect. It is offered to the pressure of every ambition—from the highest to the most utilitarian—and, for want of being adapted, it takes pleasure in sifting students according to criteria of its own creation. The less it is *operative* with respect to sociocultural expectations, the more it becomes *discriminatory*, channeling students' passage from the present toward the future into a bottleneck. Insofar as it is shown to be incapable of being a laboratory that produces a popular culture by proportioning methods to questions and needs, it becomes a filter that opposes a "discipline" to pressures exerted from the outside.

Even the meaning of admission changes. Formerly, it meant a state of fact, that is, the relationship the society had with a university that welcomed only an elite. Today, the expanded, massified university sees itself assuming the role assigned to discrimination. The culture that a small number had formerly constructed *becomes* the mechanism of discrimination applied to the masses of students.

Especially urgent is whatever can provide the university with its properly cultural role—a role that, paradoxically, it allows to escape, that it even renounces when it refuses to posit it in its present form, that is, in terms of popular culture; it does not take seriously, in view of its real policies of admission, the new task that has thus been assigned to it in the nation.

In its individual aspect, this problem can be placed under the sign of what students in North America call the "relevance" (or "pertinence") of instruction.

> In some studies, this term designates the fact of being actively involved with those who are studying what they are with a sense of meaning and not merely of utility. "Relevant" studies are those that offer an interest, a meaning, or whatever is in a real relation with those engaged in course work, and always in an apparent, manifest, evident way. In the midst of their studies, students are continually asking, "What does it mean? What is being said? How and why?"[5]

The same holds true for a large majority of French students when, in the name of admissions, they actually refuse the nonsense of an instruction unrelated to the experience it ought to clarify, far removed from the concerns that expect from it instruments of analysis, and so poorly adapted to students' abilities that the teaching might otherwise locate and make clear in the language of social communication. Culture remains absurd when it ceases to be the language—the product, the tool, and the regulation—of those who speak it; when it is used as a weapon of social discrimination and a razor of division turned against its users; when the surgical operation (of sifting and of *admitting*) wins out over cultural production (*"learning for the sake of learning"*).

In short, when the university expands its admissions and recruitment policies, it ascribes its own definition to culture. It refers an established *knowledge* to a *practice* of thought, and it sends the conceptual *objects* it mobilizes back to the *subjects* who are producing them.[6]

A Rupture: Scientific Research and the Massification of Recruitment

Although necessary, is this labor possible? In any event, it cannot be resolved according to the preestablished norms that have controlled the education of professors of this generation and that often today help them maintain their own model in the name of "culture" (what it has been, but what it no longer is), by merely aiming at training future professors who conform to the system that establishes the law of the reproduction of the same and wants what is the same to indefinitely engender the same.

It would be folly to characterize current research in the name of this cultural Malthusianism and this nostalgia for stasis. Current research represents a thousand experiments that would be impossible to summarize here. But a particularly interesting case might allow us to better perceive the nature both of the difficulties being encountered and of the problem itself.

In order to form the thirteen Parisian universities chartered by the decree of March 21, 1970,[7] regroupings of professors and disciplines were carried out. Political sympathies and collectively identical reactions with regard to the "crisis" [of May 1968] were, moreover, often as determinative as the question of studies and developing students. On the one hand, the distribution and combinations of credits has resulted in a "card game" — as one professor put it — a game of great lords whose "cards" are the masses of students. From this still very abstract notion of credits, cut out of the sky over Paris but deprived of any place of their own, and combined independently of a student "clientele" whose allocation would remain to be specified, one of the most interesting universities is Paris-VII. The most "open" of the CHU (University Hospital Centers) are part of it,[8] and, on the other hand, according to *Le Monde*, "included are a good number of progressive teachers who did not want to be associated with the universities that were considered 'reactionary' (notably Paris-IV and Paris-VI)."[9]

A university has to be created and its cursus defined; the beginning of the 1970 academic year and the orientation of students have to be foreseen; structures have to be specified, and the elections to the constituent assembly of the university remain to be prepared. A publication with a circulation of several thousand copies is attempting to follow up and to circulate the projects and the givens: *Paris-VII — Informations*. As of now, at Paris-VII problems are emerging that were born of a certain unanimity in the quest for new formulas, especially in areas where questions involve articulating the disciplines being represented and associating theory with practice.

First of all, the admissions policies suddenly appear to be the price of research. Innovations are permitted because Paris-VII is destined to be a "light" university, a play school of little consequence compared to the others. They thus imply an exploitation of the principle of *rarity*. The initial hypothesis, which has since been abandoned, only entailed the C^2 (a technical exercise that is part of the master's program, with the aim of assuring that the student has been initiated into a scientific specialty). A greater degree of specialization will be required. Recruitment will be limited; class schedules will be heavier. The newest projects in fact require a greater technical background. The level is raised and the number of participants diminished. The most innovative university is being tilted in the direction of the most rigorous selection and is being led toward an organization that resembles an elite institution, a Grande École. It follows that the pluridisciplinary garden, pruned in the virgin forest of the university, makes manifest a redoubtable *contradiction between research and massification,* as if the former were possible only thanks to the establishment of an elite among the students, through a strategy of hyperselection. Inversely, wherever it is accepted (in other universities), massification seems to bring about a return to authoritarian formulas and to lecture courses, and to involve disciplines whose resolutely more "classical" form and content consign students to silence.

On the other hand, even at Paris-VII the margin of research is limited by the fact that channels among different universities and the identity of levels or of degrees granted need to be safeguarded. With the totality of universities making up an overly homogeneous and unitary system, the options permitted to each of them remain limited. As one of the chairs reminded us, innovations must never compromise the difficult operation of assigning students to different Parisian universities at the beginning of the 1970 school year, and hence the possibility of "displacing" the student population according to the capacities of each regional branch. Once again, in the very order of research a Malthusianism prevails: the requirement of uniformity paralyzes every initiative.

In every UER,[10] and even in every seminar, this contradiction between scientific innovations and the massification of recruitment becomes part of every teacher's experience. From our point of view, it would require a solution, located at the nexus of pedagogy and of technical investigation, that *could have oriented research toward popularization.* Put differently, technical innovation would have to be made proportionate to the pedagogical relationship; the labor inhering in scientific discourse would have to have scholarly research as a model; popularization at the "elementary" level of the first cycles of study would have to cease being the opposite of research, or merely its "application," in order to become the very terrain of scientific experiment and the form of the questions being posed.

The success gained in areas where interdisciplinary innovation and teaching intersect is well known, for example, in the seminars that Jacques Dubois and Joseph Sumpf have led on innovation in teaching methods thanks to linguistics, the application of research on speed reading in university teaching, the research of the center of "educational sciences" at Vincennes, the analyses of history presented in manuals...[11]

But results are impossible wherever the problem is envisaged only on the basis of disciplines and individual teachers. From that point on, it only remains to seek the maximum flexibility for projects developed in professorial commissions, in order to include the greatest number of students. In reality, stretched beyond all limits, these projects return to their original form. And the teachers are now divided according to this rift between teaching and research, which leads them to abandon both teaching in general and teaching that constrains them to forsake all research. This is a dramatic alternative, which always takes for granted the fixed point of an established science that is *kept* or abandoned.

Numbers, a Source of Heterogeneity

We can begin with the other term of the pedagogical relationship and grasp the question in the form of the difficulty around which all of the projects making up the scholarly cursus turn, especially as far as the first cycle is concerned: the cultural heterogeneity of the student population. Here we face another aspect of the alternative: either circumscribe a discipline by authoritarian means in order to defend it from being "secondarized" or relegated to a minor status, along with strictly defined rules of control that function in accord with "correct" disciplinary space (that is, foreign to the student), or promote a free work of collaboration by withdrawing the possibility of upholding or controlling the way in which the participants (too numerous to be monitored on an individual basis) obtain suggestions or information given in the course of their exchanges. But this requires closer analysis.

Formerly, a relative homogeneity characterized those attending a lecture course or participating in a seminar. This fact was due to a slight porosity between social classes, to a rather rigid professional compartmentalization (linked to that of schools and colleges), and to the means used to sift students as they entered universities that themselves were inscribed into the continuity of secondary studies already deemed severe and arranged in accord with public functions.[12]

This time has passed. The greatest degree of heterogeneity rules among students, through their family origins, their milieus, their readings, and their cultural experiences. The phenomenon is emphasized by the participation of adults and workers (in some seminars in education, psychology, or sociology, the average age has risen from thirty to thirty-five years). The social polyvalence reaches into secondary schools despite barriers or tricentenary habits, but it is the tide of mass culture that is flooding the wetlands of the university.

In itself new and promising, this fact presents some fundamental and still often poorly analyzed conditions. Thus, the use of language is not common. Although a style and a dialect are inaugurated on different campuses, with a vocabulary and a syntax of their own, the *relationship to language* is not homogeneous (varying insofar as an idiom is a referent or an element of research), and no longer the model of its functioning.[13]

What I would like to call a *metaphorization of language* is produced at the same time and is no less visible. Just as the rationalization of mass communication has as its counterpoint a growing uncertainty about the personal use made of common language and the meaning that is ascribed to it by its receivers (what is the *same* film for a Parisian, Rhodesian, or Cameroonian public?), so then a common meaning cannot be attached to the most widely held themes and to the most objective elements of students' language. They acquire a metaphorical function, a *variable second meaning* that is, however, whatever is most likely and whatever depends on an "inner" use, in the same way that colonized peoples distort the language of the colonizers on different registers and with ironic or shifted meanings.

A sign of this mutation of stable languages into "manners of speaking" of things, political discourse *can* thus designate, by means of judgments about society, an objective situation inside the university,[14] or else, through an apologia for action, the contrary of action, that is, the impossibility of acting in which university structures control students, or yet again, through an apparent exile outside of scholarly problems, an appeal for meaning with regard to studies, and so on. The teacher has to watch out for words in the very places where he or she would like to take them seriously. The teacher can never count on them, nor attribute to them a univocal meaning established by an academic code.

Another example: student culture is becoming *kaleidoscopic*.[15] It is a puzzle. Not poor, but anomic, the culture is thus the magnifying glass of received instruction and of the real relation that exists between courses and disciplines. In this respect, it reveals the nature of the university, of this former "cosmos" that today has been fragmented and scattered into dispersed types of research in which students now wander. And if the instructor comes from a solid ground (his or her specialty) in order to envision a horizon broad enough to include other sectors of research, the same does not always hold for students entering this multiform workplace not knowing what existed beforehand, without any essential references, and with endless curiosity continually solicited by the expansion of research in all cardinal directions or by the incoherent requirements that professors have established. From this standpoint, university instruction adds its own effect to the multiplicity of information and images that propel mass culture. Instruction does not order them; rather, it adds to them. It does not take a decisive position with respect to mass culture, but duplicates its very form.

The culture in which the undergraduate circulates is thus often cumulative and anthological. It develops through "collages" and effects obtained by juxtaposition, but all the while inside of every specialty, in the style of an initiation that paradoxically (and vaguely) presents the discipline in its most unyielding (and ultimately, least scientific) form, university discourse carefully separates "basic books" from "popular manuals," meticulously classifies references according to their "value" in gradations made by the instructor, situates itself thanks to a distinction between the "pure" and "impure," and is thus insulated from any form of popularization. Therefore, the instructor is stupefied, as if by an almost blasphemous aberration, when the student associates, seemingly without knowing that a difference exists between the two, the best "basic book" with its "execrable" popularization. This leveling defies the hierarchization so characteristic of university codes of references.

Nonetheless, for the student it bespeaks the factual coexistence of advice coming from the professor and the solicitations coming from advertising. It corresponds to the cultural space in which the academic book sits next to popular paperbacks. It expresses a mass culture that a surface is defining, and not a hierarchization, and that combines offers, curiosities, and impressions. It also betrays what professors *are doing*, even if they are not *saying so*, when journalistic information or legends about the "trashers" modifies their angles on their practiced discipline and changes their reactions vis-à-vis their students. From this point of view, the uproar itself also refers to the student's own cultural anomie and makes manifest what teachers translate only through their denials or their silence.[16]

Cultural Production

Teachers are mistaken when they invest their intellectual courage in the urgency of *holding to* an accepted discourse. In that way they risk not making themselves understood and missing the mark of their basic goal, which is at once pedagogical and disciplinary. They do not make themselves understood because, in believing that they speak in the name of a "higher" knowledge (by its origins and its references), they *in fact* buy into an accumulative system in which their affirmation cannot obtain the meaning that they confer on it. If they are thus heeded (but no longer "heard"), it is only because they are inevitable and necessary, like the guardians of the portals to examination rooms and everything that stands behind them. But, constrained to live through these conditions, their auditors also are aware of the futility of their discussions with the teacher. In many universities, it can be observed that students really appear to refuse to speak up. Their silence spreads. What's the use of speaking if one is no longer being heard? And from then on, what remains to be done in course work, if not a nauseating resignation or violence whose forms and ideological justifications the majority of students recognize but disapprove of?

Especially, through their tactics of "courage" and their will to stick to values patented by the academy (and by their own training), teachers put themselves in the situation of understanding neither the figure that the expression of meaning takes in this context nor the demands that go along with it.

For often, with his or her cultural baggage, a student moves ahead in the style of collages that are made elsewhere as an individual "bricolage" or handiwork of several sound recordings or a combination of "noble" paintings with images taken from advertising. Creativity is the act of reusing and recombining heterogeneous materials. Meaning is tied to the significance that comes from this new use. This meaning is nowhere stated for itself; it eliminates all "sacred" value to which a given sign would be accredited. It implies the rejection of every object said to be "noble" or "permanent."[17] It is thus affirmed with decency, all the while bearing a figure of blasphemy. Raw material of the university could never be given a privileged status by dint of the fact that it originates from the writer of a dissertation, a "strong thesis," or the long duration of a scholarly investigation.

Central here is the cultural *act* that is part and parcel of the "collage," the invention of forms and combinations, and the procedures that allow such composite shapes to be multiplied. A *technical* act par excellence. Attention is thus directed toward practices. It is hardly astonishing to see students' interest move from *products* of research to *methods of production*. From this standpoint, the shift resembles what happens in scientific and literary domains. But the student is frustrated insofar as the teacher spends (kills) time in *exposing results*, but not in explaining *how*, in the course of a collective praxis, they are obtained — a question that would enthrall every student.

To be sure, teachers would thus be submitting their results to a critical public, in a relation homologous to what they keep with their "colleagues." But, in that way, they do not impede the future of acquired products; they open it. Further, they fail to respond not only to a question that essentially bears on their methods, and to a pedagogical task proportioned to the multiplicity of creations that can affect a cultural raw material that today is almost limitless; in a word, they not only fail to adapt to the question "what can we do with this?" but they are located exactly where the most decisive investigations take place, where new scientific (literary, sociological, psychological, etc.) *practices* are developed, where they can be verified, criticized, and confronted — in the way, for example, that the historiographer discovers the blank slate of the peasant world in our own history and attempts to discover *techniques* of analysis other than those invented by clerics, the beneficiaries who privilege the literary or written document. The historiographer is on both the terrain of research and the turf where students are taught.

This coincidence — but is it really a coincidence? — offers the possibility of marrying a pedagogy in step with the massification of the university to the requirements of scientific research. Along these lines, teaching would have as its principle less a common content than a *style*. It would not be incompatible with the heterogeneity of knowledges and the experiments among students (as among students and teachers) since it would be defined in each instance by an *operation* in which the professor would be the adviser-engineer, and thus the action perfecting methods tracing technical possibilities through mass culture.

This perspective has been opened up in law schools with the notion of TP [*travaux pratiques*], or "practical labors," and in fact, in many seminars — when the TP are not only exposés or applications of established knowledge, but the apprenticeship of methods, a textual practice, the experiment and experience of cultural fabrications and styles or "ways of doing." Workers who participate in a study on the history of the politics of labor unions can, in the name of their own experience as militants, collaborate in the tasks of the group that is *making* history, confront the discourse that has been put before them in their union with the means by which historiography is scientifically produced; they can also find in the work, with their student or worker coequals, a technique of reflection both on society and on their own options.

In this way the leisure school (*scholè* means leisure) becomes a needed labor in a technocratic culture. It sets in place an *act* producing meanings and a means for finding a place in the center of the luxurious array of a civilization that seems to put its clients in the position of voyeurs and consumers (an ultimately untenable position) and to make them increasingly passive as more and more information gets crammed down their throats.[18]

Autonomy: A Lure

A conviction, and almost an academic reflex, bars communication from the world of labor: that of an *autonomy* rooted in the tradition of a university *body*. It is translated in institutions and in privileges as conceptions of knowledge. It creates barriers and "distinctions," and it probably explains to a large degree the atrophied development of the IUT (Instituts Universitaires de Technologie [University Technological Institutes]), whose recruitment in 1973 represented a twentieth of all students (33,000 in IUT as against a total of 633,000), whereas their North American equivalents, community colleges, regrouped a third of all students (447,000 as opposed to 992,000 in traditional colleges and universities).[19] In question is not only a discreditation of professional culture with respect to university culture, the force of social prejudice, or enough credits accorded to the IUT, but also the tacit or explicit wish to *preserve* the *autonomous* evolution of a type of university instruction and to situate outside of systems of production the so-called disinterested enterprise that wastes human beings, forces, and money in order to safeguard the culture of the privileged classes. Cultural production is not possible in a system that in the name of autonomy places itself in the margins of the economic and social laws of national advancement.

This structure is now nothing more than a fiction. In the area of political problems, Paul Ricoeur stressed the issue before he left [his position as dean of] the University of Paris-XI (Nanterre) and in his letter of resignation. The fundamental problems of the university crystallized those of the entire nation. In that it "cannot be reformed in a society that refuses reform,"[20] it would be impossible to "have the university authorities shoulder the responsibility of resolving, by way of a call for force, a problem that the state in effect refuses to resolve by purely political means."[21] Inversely, the university cannot be thought of as autonomous. The university is a place where political forces are exercised, but it does not figure as one of them. Why, then, hold to the juridical fiction that dates to the time when the nation was constituted as a sum of "bodies" when, now, it no longer protects—and not even the universities—against all kinds of interventions, and it has as its only effect that of justifying arrested mentalities, discouraging innovation, and facilitating political or academic alibis?

The same condition holds, as we have seen, from the cultural point of view. Were the subject so particularly delicate and complex, there would have to be envisaged in the same perspective university "franchises" that allow instructors to leave their positions, individually choose their itineraries on the moving grounds of the UER, or go in the direction of overlapped designs that the students (that is, the nation of tomorrow) will have to accept. There, too, this power is in part a fiction, for, on the one hand, it is subject to pressures from without (and, consequently, to forces that are not shown in their true nature) and, on the other, it is linked to the irresponsibility of its beneficiaries in view of the nation. The reproach that must be made to these beneficiaries is not that they exist, but that they are masks or that they become instruments of knee-jerk reactions that preclude them from being critical or promoting relations of force wherever they let them pass for affirmations of meaning.[22]

Also swimming in the waters of popular culture, the university is in a position in which teaching is impelled to be an *act of production* and in which the student has to be a *laborer*. As Ernest Bloch-Lainé has shown, it is possible only if, when combined with the world of labor, the university can admit more workers and students can participate more, part-time, for example, in the tasks and responsibilities of professional work.[23] An identical hypothesis is linked to the most fundamental demand of May 1968: the erasure of the *isolated* category of the student or professor (distinguished from that of the "worker"), with a view toward a homogenization in labor. What is being called the introduction of popular culture in the university is the birth of the student worker and the working teacher, the abolition of the social divisions of labor. "All instructors therefore must admit for themselves the need to seek their knowledge *elsewhere,* and that to do so, they must engage *something other.*"[24]

Chapter 5
Culture and the Schools

The Content of Teaching and the Pedagogical Relation

The resistances met by the Rouchette report on the teaching of French already made it clear, in their extreme vivacity, that a change of content can call into question an organization of secondary school and culture.[1] Thus, when it replaces a historicizing justification of French with a description of the synchronic coherence of the language, the report destructures and restructures a lived relation with the mother tongue. The same holds true for other areas. In a high-school class, when Brecht is taught in place of Racine, the relation of teaching in an authorized tradition is modified through a tradition that is received for us, tied to fathers and to "noble" values. With the change is introduced a nexus of political issues contrary to the cultural model that had established the schoolteacher as a handmaiden of popular culture.

Two or three cases illustrate well the sociocultural implications of changes at work in the content of teaching. The first is the myth of originary Unity associated with the purity of language: *good* French is held to be engraved in the books of time past. Unity is the treasure locked into the past and in writing, whose masters are its depositories. The Rouchette plan shatters these Tablets of Law (in this respect it is not the first) through a return to the "free exercise of the language." We have to go further back. Today, French is spoken in Canada, Belgium, Algeria, Morocco, sub-Saharan Africa, Libya, and so on. There are several kinds of French, not a unique or single French. The current plurality has to be part of its teaching if an analysis is to be proportioned to the linguistic experience of communication. Even in France every school has been the site of exchanges between foreigners who speak different forms of French, but these exchanges lack the technical instruments to make them clear: teaching tends to excommunicate differences and "recognizes" only one form of French expression. The others are bastard children lacking social status and scientific legitimacy.

We thus face the interference of a sociopolitical norm contrary to the rigor of scientific description. An abusive process of elimination is set in place. The instructor's French always seems to aim at preserving the fetish of a unitary language, both time-tested and chauvinistic, of "received" authors, of a social category, of a favored region. This language of the instructors denies reality. It corresponds neither to the French spoken in schools nor to the French spoken elsewhere. Safeguarding "purity" wins out over the need for exchange. The education that imposes a French model forbids a cultural initiation into the differences among Francophones. It has, I believe, simultaneously contracted an allergy to the internal diversity among different ways of speaking French and an indifference, too, to other languages.

It is clear that changing the content, getting out of this ossified French of schoolbooks, the property of a milieu, the prisoner incarcerated in the hexagon, means getting at a fundamental aspect of culture, of folding another cultural behavior into French. In fact, it means accepting the shattering of language into diversified but articulated systems; thinking French *in the plural*; introducing the relation with the other (Francophone or foreign French) as a necessary condition of learning and linguistic exchange; replacing the preservation of a legislative Origin, whose magistracy is controlled by grammar books, with a multiplicity of up-to-date practices.

An adjoining problem also concerns matters of content, the relative place accorded to the *written* and to the *spoken*. A relation between them is postulated by the importance that teaching accords to orthography. From a cultural point of view, to bestow privilege upon orthography means bestowing privilege upon the past.

With orthography, etymology triumphs; that is, the origins and the history of the word are victorious. It prevails over language as it is spoken. Orthography is an orthodoxy of the past. It is imposed with the *dictée*, the narrow but required entrance into French culture in the system that confers on writing the power of law itself. Whereas a natural language is fundamentally a spoken code, the written code is what rules. Thus, everywhere the Dictionary has been established, the arc de triomphe of written and past French, that of the "authors" of yesteryear: a "monument commemorating the dead" is planted on the desk of every schoolchild and, in turn, in every household. This memorial celebrates an "unknown," a French that has never been *spoken.* The most recent, the most scientific of all dictionaries, bears a revealing title: *Trésor de la langue française.* A technical and literary marvel, it arranges the communication between Francophones among its historical monuments.[2]

Chomsky and his disciples have long been protesting against the authority of the written word. Roberts, the American author of *English Syntax,* wrote in 1964: "Scholarly systems are generally more concerned with learning to write than with learning to speak.... Therefore, there is no doubt that speaking is the fundamental reality of which writing is a secondary symbolization." To base teaching on the principle that writing is merely a transcription—the sighting point and the trace—of speech means to be prepared to find rationality in verbal practice (speech obeys laws), instead of exiling it into a scriptural conformity foreign to the effective workings of language. In that way, another status is granted to everyday activities. They become the very ground for a theoretical reflection. The latter is situated otherwise with respect to the culture of citizens for whom the instrument of production is not language and whose product is thus not writing; it means, perhaps, also relearning how to detect in language the slippages among homonyms, phonetic circulations—jokes and games producing effects of meaning—that oral literature frequently exploits (proverbs, etc.), whose importance psychoanalysis takes as its task to exhume, and that, however, escape the scriptural classification of words according to letters.

During my first teaching experience in the United States, I was at first surprised to see the number of spelling errors that the most advanced students were committing. I had been inhabited by the horror—learned since primary school—of spelling mistakes. In fact, these American students liberated me by forcing me to learn my own history anew: for French writers of the sixteenth and the seventeenth centuries, oral speech was the first reference, and writing was its trace left on paper. Today in schools they still tell the edifying story of Malherbe going to seek French among the lock pickers around the portal of Saint-Jean in Paris, but its goal concerns justifying the inheritor of Malherbe and proscribing teachers from joining in the school of French spoken by their students in public places. A cultural code of conduct is inaugurated and expressed through the role given to writing and to speech in the content of instruction.

A last example: *representations of space* circulated through the teaching of an ancestral and pseudo-"Euclidean" geometry (in its current form, it dates from the eighteenth century). In present-day language, nothing is as fundamental (with the relations of time) as spatial organization, according to which everything "that happens" is classified, distributed, and conceived. For, as Georges-Théodule Guilbaud puts it, schools most frequently distribute the fossils of mathematics, an archaeology and a museum of this spatial discourse that makes up the basis of geometry. Here again, a change in program yields a cultural impact by introducing, for example, schemas that represent spatial actions instead of forms, or, in a more learned sphere, topology, an analysis that takes into account what is approximate (the near) in order to deal with space in terms of virtual movements or passages. Calculus, linked to a practice of space, could rejoin and specify the gestural discourses to which Descartes was already referring when he advised people to go and see artisans at work in order to discover the "order" in spatial practices.

A remaining and basic question is that of the *connection between the content of teaching and the pedagogical relation*. On this point, the Rouchette report, in my opinion, is inadequate. It modifies the object put into motion, but not the way in which its essential element of education is introduced, namely, conversation, the exchange between the student and the teacher, that is, the very experience of French as language and as communication. In reality, the plan had been developed since 1963 in the context of experimental classes that are its postulate and its support. But the role that the pedagogical relation played in it has not acceded to a theoretical level. It has been consigned to silence. From so much collaboration with students emerges only the discourse describing a program to be taught.

Therein lies a symptom of the current situation. It involves knowing whether the relation is itself productive of language or if it is the channel through which a knowledge established by masters is "passed down"; if the practice of communication must intervene as a determinant in the creation of scholarly culture, or if it will be a tactic aiming at consumers of commodities fabricated by special agencies; or still, if a rift will open up between knowledge and social relations.

Two lines of research begin to diverge: one is dedicated to contents (traditional or progressive) that specialists of a discipline have developed; the other is attached to the pedagogical relation in that it becomes the specialty of a science as such or perhaps a concrete experiment isolated from works on disciplines. The training breaks in two. More precisely, it fragments into multiple objects of study (proportionate to a dissemination of knowledges) that are not built on the very practice of the relation, devoted to an occult, subterranean life, foreign to theories but nonetheless fundamental to them. Teaching vacillates between the two terms of an alternative: either entrench itself in knowledge (which a good initiation to psychology would allow to "push through"), or, together with the students, enter into the game of relations of either force or seduction (in which the scientific discourses are nothing more than metaphors).

To the very extent that scholarly knowledge is discredited when it is replaced by more profitable types of knowledge acquired elsewhere, when it is no longer so closely linked to the law of a society, it is perceived more as the artifice that conceals the more "real" conflicts of communication. The pedagogical experience thus flows into the psychology of the group. The more that knowledge is marginalized, the more *relational* problems invade the areas it had inhabited. In many respects, it is the indication of schools playing a new role. But this tendency inspires contrary effects: a greater stiffening with respect to the traditional pedagogical *object,* or else a will to resolve, via the improvement of programs alone, the difficulties created by a new functioning of schools in society at large.

No matter what the ensuing global questions may be, in the schools themselves we cannot accept a similar rift (which I am schematizing) between knowledge and relation. This dichotomy between objective programming and personal communication is increasingly beginning to characterize society at large. Schools could be *one* of the places where it is possible to relearn the connection by way of a particular practice. Already, in a fashion that has become minor, they permit experimentation with this: they constitute a laboratory in which this social problem is somehow miniaturized, but remains visible and can be addressed (which does not mean that it can be resolved), as long as the terms are made explicit. For example, the contradiction between the content of teaching (when it involves a relation with a work, with an author, with a past, as well as with received "authorities") and the pedagogical experience (when discussion between the teacher and the student is initiated) can be analyzed there: the language of knowledge then involves a hierarchical relation that runs contrary to the language that is elaborated on the basis of exchanges. Two cultural models thus confront each other, but in conditions that allow the conflict to be "dealt with" in a common praxis. Even if this laboratory experiment in no way resolves the problems of a society, it affords *the apprenticeship of operative procedures already proportioned to the global situation,* scholarly difficulties being but one of its many symptoms.

This type of operation is neither exemplary nor generalizable. Schools are no longer the central warehouse that distributes orthodoxy in the form of social practice. At least, in this mode, they are perhaps one of the points where a connection can be made between technical knowledge and social relations, and where, thanks to a collective practice, is effectuated the necessary readjustment between contradictory cultural models. This is a limited task, but it makes schools participate in the labor of a much greater scope that is now designated by "culture."

Surely, by envisioning social problems in taking the schools as a point of departure, we are taking them up only by a short end, and we can only achieve reformist experiments. Contrary to what we were able, for a moment, to hope for in France, sociopolitical transformation will not come from the university (in the broadest sense of the term). In contrast to a liberal or utopian mode of thinking, I believe that if every revolution produces a transformation in schooling, in our case it could never be the effect of action undertaken within this scholarly institution that has always been buttressed on a power other than its own, that of the state, and is henceforth decentered with respect to the activities of the country, weakened within, and set apart from the strategic sites of social organization.

Academies of Knowledge Transformed into the Club Med?

Massification of the secondary schools and high schools—and of the university—entirely changes the content as well as the internal relations of teaching. For three years, the threat of a collapse of the institution, then the return to order, have created new phenomena.

Among teachers, a feeling of insecurity has emerged. It coexists with the consciousness of their exteriority with respect to the places where culture develops — factories, the mass media, technical centers, corporate enterprises . . . Teachers float on the surface of culture, defending themselves all the more in that they know they are becoming an endangered species. They stiffen, and they are inclined to enforce the law on the boundaries of an empire of which they remain unsure.

On the other hand, students discover the university as a soft ground that cannot support the platform of a political opposition. Two currents, indicative of another functioning of the university, are sketched out.

One, *realist,* recognizes in scholarly products an exchange-value, and not a use-value. It charges the university with the task of obtaining social advantages. In this perspective, students put their necks under the guillotine of the exam or the formalism of instruction: "It's idiotic, but it's part of the contract." They play a role that has lost all credibility. Without harboring any illusions about this subject, they refuse to invest any personal concerns that might be expressed elsewhere and that, once introduced into scholarly studies, compromise success, which is linked to the artifice of a language closed in on itself.

The other, *cultural,* is especially encountered in the sector of human sciences. It is the fact of adolescents or adults who are already wage earners (even if part-time), or who have two or three years remaining before their professional work collapses, or who, as married women, gain more freedom once their children enter school. The former go to the university to explore the areas that interest them, to look for instruments and paths of reflection, to discover new bibliographical territories, to test in a technical sense what arouses their interest. They know that whatever they do will not bring them money. Other places exist for that. From this perspective, the law imported into the university is not that of their socioeconomic demands, but that of their sense of inquiry. They push the university in the direction of leisure and culture in order to transform it into a better-organized Cultural Institution, and sometimes into a Club Med of a higher calling.

I believe that this tendency will become more pronounced and will allocate to the university a *parallel* cultural function in respect to the mass media or professional training, whereas up to now it had occupied the center of national cultural orthodoxy — hence what is

called, with a name that ultimately designates all forms of social dis-
tantiation or cultural marginalism, university-wide "leftism." For
fundamentally, the difference does not begin with political sympathies, but with two ways of using the university, which are, moreover, linked to different social recruitments: one, "realistic," aims at
economic viability, while the other, "cultural," tries to create a free
space, a political distance with regard to the costs of labor. There we
discover two traditional functions of the university, but they are out
of joint by dint of the university's marginal status in the nation's
greater socioeconomic whole.

Clearly, "cultural" demands exert a pressure. They lead, at the
"base" of the university, to very stimulating collaborations, a preference for the most exotic sectors, support for the newest kinds of experiments, or a growing allergy to the psittacism of teachers taking
refuge in the trench warfare of Verdun-style humanism of the past.
In other words, contradictory movements mark a moment of evolution that bears no reference to *a single* dominant law.

The Distortions between Supply and Demand

The university keeps complex relations with society in the form of
increasingly deregulated matters of supply and demand. If we agree
that an institution is always an organ regulating supply and demand,
it is not surprising that these regulations that are out of control and
on the verge of transformation are the symptom or the effect of a collapse of institutional structures. I will underline only a few aspects
of these types of dysfunction.

The university is managed by an anonymous and saturated administration—an enormous body, sick with inertia, opaque to itself,
living a complex life that is nowhere ever explained, that has become insensitive to higher directives, to inoculations of theory, or to
outside stimuli.

Insular in the extreme, scholarly institutions are neither subject
to rules of production common to any business enterprise, nor built
on the professional training in spheres of labor, nor in synchrony with
an employment policy. National income taxes exempt them from particular economic constraints and tie them directly, in a mode of demand, to the state that nourishes them.

The rivalry with the mass media emphasizes this economic isolation in cultural terms. Formerly with a fixed place in the official

bureau of culture, the university is "beaten" (if a metaphor from sports can be used) by networks of training and information far more consequential than its own. Henceforward, an uncertainty prevails over what can be asked of it and over what it can offer.

More than any other "body," the university, in charge of the nation's great crusades, has been the site of ideological investments. As it generally happens, these cultural models survive the circumstances they used to convey. Today, they lag behind socioeconomic evolution. But they arm and accredit the resistance to a new situation, the very analysis of which is obliterated by the repetition of the discourses that animated the campaigns of years past.

Political, financial, industrial powers, and so on, occupy the university to an increasing degree: parties, labor unions, corporate enterprise, and the military complex hold dominion over entire sectors. Like Africa in the nineteenth century, the university is a continent over which colonizers argue: between labor unions and bosses, for example, there is the Fachoda.[3] But this occupation is not accompanied by the responsibilities that devolve upon instruction. It is an infiltration. It saps the university's "autonomy" without running the risk of putting itself in the place of the pseudo-"authorities" it exhibits on its stage. The marketplace of supply and demand is rigged when nobody can can know for sure who is responsible for what.

Concurrently, when secondary schooling loses its force, a broad field of opinion asks it to solve two of the most serious problems of contemporary society: a redefinition of culture, and an integration of youth into it. Greater ideological demands and frustrations are thus passed on to scholarly institutions. Yesterday's society used to include a plurality of ideological groups, such as political organizations, social formations, churches, and youth movements. A desert of credibility follows on the heels of this proliferation, at the very site where forces have survived their beliefs and where they still exploit them (but for ends that have more to do with advertising than with programmatic concerns). So the university is often seen responding to the unjust reproach of embodying, more than other institutions, this ideological vacuum, or the exorbitant requirement of filling the void. Witnesses to a global mutation in all frames of reference, teachers are often the prisoners of this claim, but are also complicitous with the reproach insofar as they harbor the illusion of believing that they have or ought to have "values" to distribute.

From this bleak picture (but it has to be painted) it is now incumbent upon us, I believe, to rethink and to resituate secondary schooling as a function of the actual relations between supply and demand.

In the past, scholarly culture made a point of being disinterested, but it could do so because it was based on a solid ground of power. Instruction in the nineteenth century was backed by the power of the French Republic, by lay organizations, and so on. It clearly bore a certain disinterest, but only insofar as it created a space of work not immediately allotted to a profession or to a power. This space was nonetheless conditioned by the existence of a power and was destined to "reproduce" it.

Today, the assurance that this disinterested culture used to represent appears to be lacking. Among instructors in both lower and higher education one sees the conviction or the suspicion that power is no longer behind them. Hence, another type of support is needed. In 1972, I perceive a symptom in the fact that the most active political group to which the French university teachers belong is increasingly the Communist Party. Two aspects of this new tendency are striking. First, the Communist Party can offer French intellectuals an ideological frame of reference that can replace what formerly went in the name of patriotism, secular forces, scientism, positivism, whereas power is unable to provide any of these (De Gaulle had been a surfeit of its signifiers, and Pompidou its rarity). On the other hand, since university teachers are always backed by a power, they basically have to remain in the role of functionaries. But since the base of support that until now political power maintained is lacking or is becoming inadmissible, a constituted force is being sought in the Communist Party.

Since the sixteenth century, the teaching body always needed this double reference: one to an ideology that upholds in teaching the possibility of a mission, of an evangelism; the other to a force, for the teacher has no power other than that which affects the organization of a society. This double role has been played successively by the church, then the state, and so forth. It reveals the rapport that a "disinterested" culture keeps with an "interested" or invested power.

Research, a "Political" Problem

In fact, there is a growing tension between research and teaching (popularization). On the one hand, at the budgetary level, the portion allotted to research is diminishing in all European countries, and some-times at catastrophic rates. On the other hand, in actual scholarly experience, the requirements of teaching consume almost all of the teacher's energies. In the French tradition, however, professors used to avail themselves of leisure time, which, moreover, grew as they climbed the hierarchical ladder, and which allowed them to continue to do research. This aspect of research was maintained as far down as primary education, along with its sessions and seminars devoted to pedagogy. What prevails today in university politics is the immediacy of the relation between teachers and students. The margin of criticism or of self-criticism that research used to represent is now diminished. However, the most serious problems—for example, the relations between economic development and culture—require, on the contrary, and more than ever before, urgent reconsideration. This urgency is growing as the funding earmarked for research is diminished.

The French tradition used to establish a hierarchy between research and teaching. Commissions of experts developed programs that were then diffused into the entire mass of National Education, and in the microcosm of teaching, books were taught that carried authority, that is, the product of research. Research was at the origin of a diffusion. Today, this relation is being turned topsy-turvy. At the upper levels of large institutions, what wins out is a policy based on the immediate satisfaction of needs and on administrative organization. You manage and you fill the gaps according to whatever problem comes along. In short, pedagogy or popularization is "done" while research is more finely nuanced. Yet, at the base, at the level of the smallest teaching units, research indeed is swarming in miniature laboratories and new experiments that transform both the discipline and the pedagogical relation. This is at once important and quite dangerous: very important because this time research begins from a base and rises, without elitist pretensions or a character defined from above; very dangerous because overly small experiments are too compartmentalized to obtain means sufficient enough to conduct them. Beyond a threshold marked by a financial limit, research can no longer be pursued. Furthermore, the results that are disseminated cannot be built on earlier findings. Fireflies in the night, they illuminate a little everywhere, in universities and high schools. Then, they no sooner are extinguished. I very much fear the effect of lassitude and discouragement that goes with research that is not supported by global structures of teaching.

A Critical School

Every individual experience functions within a system of economic structures. For example, the projects of permanent training at Grenoble have already inspired, on the part of employers, by a clientele of enterprises that they represent. They will thus seek to impose their norms and to use the training periods under their own purview. Experience cannot be isolated from the socioeconomic whole in which it intervenes. At no moment can a particular course of study, however autonomous, marginal, or innovative it may be, avoid the problem of its relation with existing powers.

Suffice it for us to recall the case of relations between secondary education and power. For three centuries, and especially since the French Revolution, the secondary school has been the weapon of a political centralization. It should be added that it has also been the instrument that advertises democracy, that has been displaced into the smallest of villages through a shift of its geography. Cities and towns have been "marked" by the implantation of schools: as space infused by the state, that does not conform to the environment, it is a geometrical site, like a military barracks, with square rooms and rectilinear corridors, an architectural projection of the teaching formulated within it. This temple of a unique and centralized Reason impressed the seal of a cultural power onto the village.

Today the situation is different. Cultural power is no longer localized in a school, but is diffused into every farmhouse and every room with television screens. It is "personalized." Its products are insinuated everywhere. It becomes intimate. That changes the position of the school. Formerly, as a representative of the pedagogical state, the school had as an adversary the family that played a controlling role. Every evening, when children returned to their homes, a familial readjustment was permitted with regard to the culture being taught at school. Today, the school is in an almost opposite situation: with regard to the family invaded by the televised image, it can become the site of control where are learned the uses of an information that is henceforth given outside of school. Yesterday, school was the channel that led to centralization, but today unitary information comes through the reduced area of the television tube, through advertising, through business, through publicity, and so on. And school can form a critical crux where teachers and students develop their own practices from information that has come from different sources.

To this very extent, secondary school no longer holds the same relation with power. It now battles on two fronts. It remains a state institution that the government delegates to diffuse culture defined by the center. But it also finds itself in a position at once critical and threatened with regard to the culture that mass media disseminates. This ambivalence can constitute a pole of resistance (that does not need to be contestatory). In fact, among teachers a critical spirit is developing that is first of all connected to their sociological position; it is the ideological effect of their marginal situation. Teachers are no longer at the center of culture, but on the margins. Although they depend on the ministry of a state culture, teachers can thus find ways to gain distance with regard to cultural imperialism henceforth popularized by advertising and television. A plurality of cultural points of view can thus be assured.

A Multiplicity of Cultural Places

Instruction in France is located in very diverse positions. Three can be distinguished by topographical means. First of all, it lives in an ossified world. Everywhere the administrative centralization of schooling has a paralyzing effect in the national body, a cultural latency, an extraordinary passivity. Despite the reforms that confer more responsibility on the regional academic echelons or on each high school, uniform standards continue to freeze the body of National Education.

However, various cultural porosities are evident, signs of symbiosis with the milieu, such as the agreements that envisage a permanent training, or the conventions between an enterprise or an association of industrial enterprises and a technical school or a university. At all of these points, the boundaries of the body are softened and changed. It is hard to tell where the school is located. New courses are formed that evade all "scholarly" definition. A new organization is sketched out, even if these localized changes seem for the moment to deaden the remainder of the body and make overall reform all the more difficult.

The school is not just a no-man's-land in relation to truer sites of culture. It is also an agent of transition, I would say even of transit. We see forms born, an enormous expense of energy that provokes political conflicts. One example: permanent training. Established institutions or the great fiefdoms of the political order argue over the colossal sums allocated to this sector. Each wants rewards for ongoing research in order to extend its empire or have its conceptions prevail. These struggles prove at least that things are budging.

Finally, the third site of teaching is deliberately located outside of the school. Numerous industrial, professional, union organizations, or merely specialized journals assure, exclusively for themselves, a broad training that ranges from reflection on values to technical analysis. An abundant cultural and pedagogical literature is developed on the basis of professional duties or leisure activities: fishing, gardening, home repairs . . . In my opinion, it is no less important than what scholarly manuals are publishing. They offer a pedagogy that is independent of the influence of the university, even though this production often exploits paradigms formerly developed in secondary schools. If schools can be faulted for being inert or marginal, then the culture defined by these professional or technical places can be reproached for being utilitarian. In the latter sector, culture functions as a market economy, arranged according to the trade or the type of industrial organization being promoted. It is a deliberately self-interested culture.

We are witnessing a *multiplicity of cultural places.* It is becoming possible to maintain several kinds of cultural references. With respect to the monopoly that secondary schools formerly held, a greater freedom becomes possible with this play of different cultural objects. In my view, it thus seems premature and unrealistic to suppose that secondary schooling has run its course and that cultural problems are uniquely based on professional activities, or to affirm the opposite in order to funnel back to the schools everything that is being done in the industrial or technical domains. Different cultural places represent a triangular construction that gives everyone the site of a cultural autonomy, a space of creativity. To be sure, such a "freedom" could only be illusory, for these three poles (if only they are kept in mind) are also inscribed in a system that, by becoming homogeneous, turns their differences into fictions. In spite of everything, the rigid structure of French pedagogy appears to be increasingly replaced by a plurality of institutions grounded on political and economic conflicts. Industry would like to place it entirely in its own hands; National Education does not want to lose hold of traditional teaching and seeks to bring permanent training back home to roost. Work needs to be done to ensure that an even more oppressive monolith does not result, and to bring about the genesis of plurality.

To a great degree, culture is excommunicated from pedagogy. For example, professional activities (except for a few so-called liberal ones) are not assumed to be cultural. In the IUT, a trade is learned, and to it are added a few classes in philosophy or in general culture foreign to professional activity. A little bit of patent culture is lacquered over technical activity that, nonetheless, in itself remains a fundamental site of culture.

Surely if it is true that any human activity *can* be cultural, it is not necessarily or is not yet inevitably recognized as such. If culture is really going to exist, it is not not enough to be the author of social practices; these social practices need to have meaning for those who effectuate them. Formerly, this accession of action to meaning was facilitated by religion, which ascribed meaning to the slightest of everyday gestures. To plow a furrow, to craft a chair, to drive a mill wheel, religion used to assert, has real meaning. Socialism, patriotism, and other great integrative convictions have since assured what religion once represented. But is this still true today? Now the risk of meaning is *exposed*, but without the protection of an encompassing ideology.

But must this risk at least be possible? Hence a monolithic culture impedes creative activities from becoming meaningful. It still dominates. Real, clearly dominant activities are culturally silent, and are not recognized. The role of being "the" culture is attributed to a given compartmentalized mode of social practice. To the detriment of others, the burden of culture is borne on the shoulders of a minor category of creations and social practices. Entire sectors of experience are thus deprived of the qualities that would allow them to assign meaning to their activities, their inventions, and their creativity.

No special places exist in society to which all others can be furnished with what grants meaning to them. This would be equivalent to restoring the unitary model of a religion imposed on everyone—a state ideology or the "humanism" of a colonizing class. What group has the right to define in the place of others what must have meaning for them? Surely culture is more than ever, in the hands of power, the means of granting, now as before shrouded under a "human meaning," a form of state reason. But culture in the singular has become a political mystification. Furthermore, it is deadly. It menaces creativity itself. Today, a new problem is more than likely to be one of finding ourselves before the hypothesis of a plurality of cultures, that is, of systems of references and meanings that are heterogeneous in relation to each other. To the homogenization of economic structures there must be a corresponding diversification of cultural expressions and institutions. The more the economy unifies, the more culture must be variegated. It cannot be said that we are succeeding, nor even that we are really heading in the right direction. But is it possible otherwise to maintain that, in the last resort, the meaning of existence is identical to the many shapes that the risk of being human really requires? That is a signifying practice, a meaningful practice. It consists not in receiving, but in positing the act by which each individual *marks* what others furnish for the needs of living and thinking.

Chapter 6
Minorities

Political or Cultural Manifestos?

The registers by which a minority movement can be formed are cultural and political. The danger that needs to be underlined is the risk of being forever lost in either the one or the other, either solely the cultural or solely the political.[1]

The difficulty that a certain number of minority movements are facing is one, in a first wave, of being located negatively. A cultural, social, or ethnic autonomy always draws attention to itself by saying *no*: No, says the black, I am not American. No, says the Indian, I am not a Chilean or an Argentinian. No, says the Breton, I am not French. That is an absolutely basic beginning, but it very quickly becomes deceptive if we stick to it, since we risk identifying both with a political ideology and an exclusively cultural formulation.

I am stating *political ideology* because minorities do not possess any real political force, at least as long as centralizing structures are maintained that eliminate the social possibility for minorities to express themselves in their own right. We thus fall back into ideology and into discourse.

On the other hand, the most immediate form of expression is of a cultural order. Breton manifestos state: "We have other traditions, we refer to another history, we have other forms of communication, and so on." But if we only stick to this cultural element, we will be fatally taken over from one day to the next, and precisely because cultural expression is only the surface of a social unity that has not yet been given its own political and cultural consistency.

To hold fast to this cultural presentation means buying into the society that constituted cultural elements as spectacle and as folkloric objects of an expanding economic and political enterprise. From then on, if we identify with a cultural representation, we are caught in a national "theater" in which the players would be—and this is oddly funny—Bretons, Occitans, Catalans, and so on, who are aligned with drug addicts or leftists. By seeking to attest to something autonomous, whenever it wishes to be marked by a cultural definition, cultural expression is deceived on the very ground on which it is situated. Furthermore, at the level of this cultural expression, we can easily see how so much time is spent by contradicting oneself. A very interesting article by Jean Larzac is a case in point.[2] He protests against the assimilation of Occitania into French history. How does he go about it? He refers everywhere to French chronology. He says, for example: "The defeat of Muret, our Waterloo"; "Montségur, our Oradour," and so on. In fact, the reference is French and only its negative can allow Occitan history to be silhouetted. In a first wave, how could it ever be otherwise? This Occitan history can only remain to be written in the language of the other that it inverts. But as long as one remains at that logical level, one is soon in an empty position. Occitan history indicates a place, but in a second wave, it needs to be filled. It has to be filled through a real political act. Only a power will allow speech to be taken on its own account, to speak on its own behalf.

There we have a basic problem because, in a broad sense, cultural claims are often tied to a wider economic and political dependency. In Quebec, in Occitania, or in Brittany, the progressive disappearance of an economic independence (upheld by the very isolation of rural areas) and the progress of centralization force autonomy to flow back toward cultural matters. In this respect, cultural claims appear to be a remainder and a compensation.

That is combined with another, apparently contrary, phenomenon. There had to be (a rather relative) enrichment of the French in Quebec, or a promotion of peasant directors in Brittany (in cooperatives, in the city offices, etc.), in order for demands for autonomy to appear. In getting out of their isolation, by entering into the play of political or economic structures, the Quebecois or the Bretons have noticed that their promotion was being arrested at a threshold, that it was bumping into the doors of the offices of those holding power in higher places. Their promotion allowed a consciousness to be raised. It brought the forces of represssion that until then had been invisible—or less visible when nothing was threatening them—out of the shadows.

But this promotion also threatens the very people who are its subjects. In many regions it assimilates new generations into the culture pushed ahead by the economic structures in which the people are entering. The traditional points of reference (in language, custom, family) recede, disappear, and on occasion become extinct: the use of a language of one's own is localized in marginal activities, it is relegated to the periphery, and sometimes wastes away. This disappearance makes identification difficult, and sometimes even anguishing or impossible. How can a Breton or an Occitan identity be found when the points of reference that were given to parents or to grandparents are eradicated or obsolescent? Only then is there a brutal return to local tradition, to a local language, but it is a return to something that has already become foreign. We return to something that still inhabits us (a means of identification), but it has already become other or altered.

Something analogous is happening in what Edgar Morin noted about Plodémet.[3] "Breton consciousness" has a lot to do with a cultural concoction. Thus, up to the First World War, villages (I am not speaking of parlimentarians or of bourgeois) were identified by being distinguished from one another. In the years 1914–18, villagers arriving in barracks saw themselves being treated as "Bretons" by Parisians or other provincials. They gained a self-consciousness as "Bretons" at the very moment when they were mixed together with non-Bretons. The feeling of being different is tied to the designation of this difference by others, and to a situation that in its "French" solidarity continued to diminish lived autonomy.

In other words, cultural claims are not a simple phenomenon. The itinerary normally taken and followed by a movement that defines autonomy begins by exhuming — corresponding to a first wave of consciousness-raising — the political and social implications bound within it. It is not tantamount to eliminating the cultural reference simply because the capacity of symbolizing an autonomy at the cultural level is needed for a real political force to appear. But only a political force is going to furnish cultural expression with the effective power of affirmation.

We are touching on one of the points that, in my view, is gaining importance, namely, how can a real, effective political organization be drawn from a cultural demonstration? I believe it can be done only by being rid of the idea of a cultural enclave, the idea that the problem involves Bretons and Bretons alone. If Basques and Bretons

have been unable to win autonomy, it is because of the global organization of the society in which they live. In this sense, their problem
concerns all French citizens; at stake is the impossibility imposed on
each and every person to live in a society that admits a plurality of
groups. Bretons are thus positing—but with reinforced vigor—an
issue that affects any group that lives within the borders of French
society. If the question is no longer that of a democracy of political
groups, and is reduced to a cultural demonstration of a few French
citizens, the non-Breton groups will be recognized in Brittany as nothing more than folklore.

In other words, we cannot mistake a symptom for the malady.
Thus, in Brittany there are the leftovers of a tradition of its own that
are the indication of an autonomy that remains visible among its inhabitants, but these leftovers are not at all the reality of the question.
If we look closely at the symptom, then a folklorization of Brittany
will become apparent, at least of its Breton element. Another phenomenon will be produced, perhaps even more dangerous: in order to
"become" Breton, Bretons will perceive no means other than to "go
in reverse," to regress toward their past. Bretons will only amount to
an object in a museum of their own if their only political, social, or
other point of reference to their autonomy is what it was in their past
or what is being eradicated. On the contrary, insofar as Bretons can
recognize in these cultural symptoms a problem that calls them to
assume a new position in respect to French society as a whole, insofar as other (non-Breton) formations must also be born in this society; insofar as cultural claims can also take the form of a political
struggle against social or cultural centralization—only from that moment can the Breton question no longer be reduced to its past, nor to
a national object of folklore.

*But then, doesn't this global restructuring of society that you're trying to
envisage amount to a juxtaposition of groups that only seek their autonomy?*

There, in my opinion, you hit the nail on the head of a global problem that goes beyond French society. We are currently witnessing a
general evolution. Large national structures that used to defend interest groups or individuals (labor unions for workers, universities
for students, local offices for citizens) are now subject to the law of
centralization. In its internal organization, each one of these units in-

creasingly conforms to the laws of a given enterprise, and in its relations with others it becomes increasingly dependent on a central power. Local magistrates now find themselves occupying the position of functionaries. The autonomy of the body of magistrates has become a fiction: the police or the prefecture increasingly determines the position of the magistrates, whereas in other times the magistrates made up a body with its own force, a body capable of defending a certain number of rights and demands, and possessing an autonomy. In the same way, the university for a long time had been an autonomous body; now it is a flabby body, a colony occupied by external powers, such as the Communist Party, the French right, and the financial interests of powerful technocracies. It no longer exists as an autonomous body. The same can be said for a certain number of labor unions that have become commercial enterprises of their own and manage a force in a general system of the economy, but that have abandoned representing their own constituency. Inside of a labor union we are witnessing the same laws that are at play inside the French conservative party or in other organizations.

With respect to this leveling and this homogenization of socioeconomic structures, social units of another kind are now visible, units that are not yet entirely organized. Their expression is found with youth movements (which are not exactly those of students because they rightly challenge the division between students and workers, although with difficulty, but at least the problem is raised), or with groups of consumers, ecological factions, and so on. Something else is coming out of the ground: new social forms have to be constituted in relation to each other, but according to a plurality of powers. This forever obscure genesis is currently being repressed; it is repressed by a central political power that simultaneously depends increasingly on great financial and technocratic powers. Ethnic minorities are putting onto the agenda precisely a problem of this nature, but in a different way. Clearly, there is a difference of quality between these social units. Feminism is not the Breton problem, nor is it that of the consumer. But meetings and analogies dot the horizon. They tend to constitute a plurality of noncentralized groups and pose the global problem of the structure of society. Local interests are forbidden wherever neither labor unions, political parties, nor universities have success. Thus minorities are today opening up a *general* question that concerns the type of our societies. This problem must not disappear

under its initial expression, nor let itself be relegated to regional identity by centralizing powers that break the links of pressure groups
that as a unit can call a general system into question.

*Do you think that ethnonational demands ought to play a specific role
in the growth of this multiplicity of minority demands, and of demands for
autonomy?*

Yes, entirely. With respect to the movement that marked the second
half of the nineteenth century and the first half of the twentieth, and
that drew the peasantry and the provincials toward Paris or toward
urban centers (the flow went from the country to the city, from the
provinces to the capital), we are beginning to observe a backward
surge in many societies. American cities, for example, are witnessing
the evacuation of their centers as the middle classes move to the suburbs, in ways that the line drawn between the city and the country
now becomes a subject for achaeologists. In this posturban society,
we are increasingly discovering in the urban core the most proletari-
anized groups and, in the "countryside" of not long ago, the richest
and most technocratic strata. We have witnessed an inversion of the
movement.

For one thing, the revival of the countryside, the renewal of
provincialisms and of a certain number of autonomies are inscribed
in this general movement. Even at the cultural level, the possibility
of envisaging the Breton problem as an important issue for French
society is tied to the economic, touristic, and middle-class ebb that I
just mentioned. That is a broader movement that prompts one to say:
"Brittany, Languedoc, Provence, well, why there's money in that!" Thus
scientific research, urbanism, history, and archaeology are increasingly
attracted to what is taking place in the provinces. This return to
those areas is a canvas on which the demands for autonomy are being painted.

But the main interest of ethnic, Occitan, and Breton minorities
entails conferring a political meaning on this return of the repressed,
this renewed interest in the provinces. It means not just letting it be
inscribed in the homogeneous movement of a technocratic flow back
to the country. Surely social categories that return to the provinces
represent an urbanization of the country. They are colonizing the totality of French territory with investments, with preoccupations, with
a type of cultural communication that had formerly been developed

in urban areas. This means that the Breton movement, by profiting to an extent from this surge coming from exteriority, wants to be posited as autonomous and not only as dependent on the city or the new interest of groups promoting development in the provinces. In other words, the Breton movement advances the issue that is eliminated through this sociotechnocratic development of the provinces within the logic of capitalist society. It envisages the problem in ways other than in the shape of an immediate relation between, on the one hand, individuals (the bourgeois or the boss who wants to move into Beg-Meil) and, on the other hand, an economic system. The Breton movement restores a necessary mediation: the intervention of the concerned local group. But then this will not always be a general law of society that attracts individuals in the direction of the provinces. There is a collective reality that belongs to Brittany that cannot be assimilated or crushed by socioeconomic laws alone.

This interference on the part of the Breton constituency as such reintroduces into economic—ultimately abstract—analysis the political desires of the members belonging to a given group. We are rightly noting in the capacity to bring to success a politicization of economic evolution observed throughout a society as a whole. The ideology of every liberal or capitalist movement usually considers social phenomena only from the angle of a general law in its relation with individual desires. It erases from history the conflicts and relations among groups or classes. It thus eliminates all collective desire. The Breton movement (which I am using here as an example) reintroduces the desire of a group of people who wish to impose, in a certain number of areas, some common choices of their own.

The Imperialism of Ethnological Knowledge

A somewhat tangential question, perhaps: the feeling is that many people, and first of all ethnologists—a case in point being Emmanuel Terray—are currently experiencing a certain difficulty in defining what is meant by "ethnic."

No, it is not a tangential question. It is fundamental. Is an ethnic group an object of knowledge, or is it what a group defines by its act? For example, there is no "negritude" insofar as it is only a collection of cultural objects or themes, an object created through ethnological analysis. Negritude exists only as of the moment when there is a new subject of history, that is, when people opt for the defiance of existing. I fundamentally believe in this definition of a group since the series of revolutions beginning with the end of the eighteenth century: a social unit exists only when it runs the risk of existing. What constitutes an ethnic group is not the fact that an ethnologist or a sociologist can somehow or somewhere define the Breton as the object of his or her interest or knowledge. This "object" is, futhermore, perpetually "vanishing"; for the a priori of the ethnological method "suppresses" the *act* by which Bretons become Bretons and speak, in their own name, as the language of their desire to live, the cultural elements analyzed by the observer. Now, an abstraction cannot be made of the act that *holds* all these objects together. Insofar as we want to define Bretons objectively, we reduce them to data described in an economic or archaeological gazetteer. *There is*, in Carnac, a particular economy; *there are* megalithic alignments of stones... But, "fundamentally," this gazetteer does not suffice. It "forgets" the essential. Here we recoup the political issues: a political unity exists only as of the moment when a group gives itself the objective and task to exist as such.

So Brittany is beginning to be born ...

Yes. But with a few of the difficulties that the events make clear, not only in Brittany, but also in other regions in which the same problems are encountered: Catalonia, French Quebec.

This unity initially appears in a cultural form because it is deprived of its own means from the standpoint of both politics and economy. In this respect, it is characteristic that these minority movements are born in the regions that have been exploited by majoritarian societies; for example, southern Italy, Quebec, Occitania have furnished to northern Italy, to central or northern France, to English-speaking Quebec, people and riches that allowed centralizing powers to move in. But today in southern Italy, as in Quebec, this oppression is recognized. The drive for autonomy thus appears as the *prise de conscience* of a repression, but by the same token it is associated with an absence of socioeconomic means to defend this autonomy.

There is no ready-made answer to this question. For example, in Occitania: what are the political and economic means available to Occitans with respect to their cultural demands? It is not difficult to see that the large commercial, chemical, and aeronautical industries around Toulouse or the political powers, through the intermediary of prefects, mayors, the police, and so on, do not belong to Occitania. Autonomism is cultural because, first of all, it is powerless. We discover a tension that is common to every instance. There can be no autonomy without struggles. Economics does not emerge from power struggles. All movements that intend to defend autonomy must prepare themselves one way or another. It is impossible to hold to a political theory developed in some central office or in cultural diffusion. These are metaphors or signs of future conflicts if we are really to take seriously the demand for autonomy.

There is a real link between ethnology and the desire for centralization and/or colonization. The colonizing countries have been and are always forces negating culture.

Ethnology is not innocent. It represents one of the forms of colonization. The interest that ethnology brings to popular culture assumes a relationship of forces between the bourgeoisie to which these ethnologists belong and the mass or the milieu that becomes the object of their gaze. The difficulty is that ethnology no longer avows, or better conceals, this relationship of forces; it takes it as a postulate. The military is obsolete. In the context of the ethnologist, it has no role since the economic and social oppressions of the whole system allow the ethnologist to develop his or her discourse without having to make clear his or her real relationship to the political and economic structure of oppression.

In a more general sense, every position of knowledge that establishes as an object a category of people implies, by definition, a relationship of force and domination. It assumes that at that very place these people are no longer subjects and citizens entirely of their own being. For example, among the blacks whom I saw in Los Angeles, Chicago, and elsewhere, a different gaze is directed toward black culture, a different analysis is made than that of the ethnology or sociology of whites. Every historiographer or ethnologist always remains the symptom or the flag of the milieu that develops it. That includes their technical methods. Thus our own historiography favors written documents, that is, it is interested only in the social category that is homogeneous with that of the author and the readers of that history. In fact, 99 percent of the population our historians talk about are illiterate. Historiographical discourse imposes as *the* history of society a tautology that always makes "the same ones" (those who write) the authors, the readers, and the privileged consumers of these studies. The "rest" is silently repressed by this circle of the "same."

Every historiography or ethnography always represents the emphasis of one power over the other. Thus it is not possible for a minority movement merely to confine itself to a political demand. It also has to change the culture. It is absolutely stunning to see, for example, how Algerian autonomy has made possible an Algerian historiography, and how the independence of Cuba has allowed the *cimarrones*, the runaway black slaves whose voices had forever been silenced and who had never participated in the creation of culture, to be introduced into the cultural discourse. The political foundation of a social unit is the condition of possibility for a new culture.

But when I speak of countries that gain political independence, I do not wish to imply that political autonomy will solve every dilemma. In a certain number of African countries, today we witness a dependence that is much greater than in the time when they had not obtained their political independence. The disappearance of costs imposed by colonization represents a savings for the colonizing countries, and considerable advantages at the level of financial investments, sales of industrial products, or commercial exchanges — thus, this is a gain for them. As Sempé says, nothing is simple.

The Idiom of Autonomy

From the point of view of cultural autonomy, does language pose an "absolute" problem? In Algeria certain people say: "Kateb Yacine amounts to nothing more than a French writer..."

That is like saying that Cuban independence would only be possible if the Cubans had constituted a local Cuban language. It is not true. Furthermore, to have had a language of one's own (that is the case today of the Bretons) risks being deceptive. Insofar as the problem is located at a democratic and political level, the Bretons are those who now have to define the cultural conditions that will allow them to be what what they want to be. The mode of expression that had once been theirs is not necessarily what will today constitute the expression of a Breton unity. Taking the Breton language as an absolute *can* risk being reactionary. It might run contrary to the evolution that is unfolding in economic and linguistic spheres and paralyze Breton progress. In Algeria, the imposition of Arabic in all areas would have led to a paralysis of scientific, technical, and cultural development; thus it was resolved to continue to teach the exact sciences in English or in French. Since its independence, Algeria has accepted—especially during its first years—a "Frenchification" of the population as a whole, precisely because literacy programs, hence the confirmation of sociopolitical autonomy, temporarily called for the introduction of French. But now an inverse linguistic movement is becoming possible. Language is a means, it is not an end on the basis of which everything needs to be judged.

In France not long ago, demands were made to eliminate *franglais,* an English vocabulary mixed with French. Is that not a reactionary demand—or a regression toward the Gallic vocabulary of past utopias? One risks giving way to the mythology of origins.

In fact, there exist many different linguistic situations. For example, the use of Breton in Brittany and the use of Catalan in Catalonia correspond to heterogeneous functionings. Catalan is spoken fluently in Catalonia, but Breton is not spoken fluently in Brittany. To wish to impose Breton as the essential sign of an autonomy would mean privileging a few old people or a few specialists. It is possible to envisage a politics of Bretonization of the language over the long term. That is what is being observed in Algeria: today the introduction of French allows a policy of Arabization of the language. A policy is characterized by linking a tactic to a strategy. Autonomy is of the order of strategy; language is of the order of tactics. It is possible, for example, that the Bretonization of Brittany is going through a moment when the Breton language is disappearing. I am not sure; the jury is still out. But, in any event, language cannot be considered as an end without turning it into a taboo. The true language of autonomy is political.

Part III

Cultural Politics

Chapter 7
The Social Architecture of Knowledge

We must provide the practical and theoretical afterthoughts to the request for a democratic creativity, or for everyone's active participation in common representations. Practical *and* theoretical: the linkage is crucial if current crises challenge the bond of power and representation, after having begun with a challenge to the disciplines that provide social life with an operative apparatus and an interpretation, a tool and and an image (psychology, sociology, etc.).

A dangerous gap between what is said and what is done calls for a labor that will not set aside either theory—political science, the study of society, economy—or conceptions of history and culture. The symbolic revolution of May 1968 has called into question the relation of theory to action,[1] whence its global character: at stake is a *totality* when the *relation of a society to its own system of representation* is put in doubt. May 1968 is not a ghost story, an image that would for a moment flicker on the screen of everyday life. A problem of structure has been revealed with a gap opened up between knowing [*savoir*] and doing [*faire*]. We are all being examined about our *conceptions,* which are suddenly covered, as if under a shadow, by the reality that they felt they were designating; a *functioning* seems to command the disciplines that until now were considered stable and determinative; a cultural *organization* is at issue with the divisions we use to develop disciplines and the divisions in which production is made—a broadening of critical scope that in May 1968 aimed at the division between students and workers. Now a new "disquiet" sends tremors through the foundation of our society.

The slippage that puts the latent and explicit layers of the nation out of touch with each other requires us to ask some global questions for which we have to muster the courage to debate; for the phenomenon that has been produced is, perhaps, telling civilization that a point of maturity has been reached, one in which the fruit bursts and is scattered, in which meaning appears to be exiled from structures, in which the quest for identity leads us far from home. Thus an ending would be heralded, and so would the beginning of something else ... It also might be that the requirement leading so many people to protest against a society and institutions that *refuse to speak the truth* is vain, either because *no* society can satisfy the requirements of this complaint, or because it can no longer be so through the one in which *we* belong, if the confidence that it had in itself and in its language disappears in order to leave only one remainder: the security owed to the commodities it produces. It is still important to distinguish between these two hypotheses.[2]

From a historical point of view, it is striking to observe once again the alternation of brief ideological revolutions that contrast with the long duration of identification with a central power. It may be a specifically French condition. The centralized "model" of Louis XIV would have been indefinitely reused later on (though in the name of different principles); France, "the land of a state tradition" — in which reign a worry over the definition of status and an (egalitarian) suspicion about "savage" initiatives, hence an establishment of strict hierarchies that favors bureaucratic centralization — would only know abrupt ruptures, of a nature too ideological and too absolute not to be compensated for and destined to failure.[3] Or else does it point to a Latin mentality, as might be suggested at once by the origins and development of democracy, which are typically northern (?), and the conflicts that underpin our modern societies, between "Roman" hierarchies and Protestant communities?

In a more sociopolitical perspective, the timeworn distinction between the "explicit" function and the "latent" function of social institutions gains a growing importance.[4] It will thus be necessary to analyze why and how their divergence develops and what it means. In the same way, the history of ideas invites reflection on the process that now reduces so many rich theories or representations to mere surface effects, deceptive signs of a reality that carries them off at the moment when they are supposed to represent it. In these methodologies of every discipline, a gap is opened up between their theory and their action. The net effect is that parties, unions, and often churches are no longer where they say they are. Recent events and facts bring all these questions forward.

A Conception of Culture: The Elite and the Mass

As an example, I would like only to envisage a conception of culture that we are also led to reexamine — one of those that determine our analysis of situations: the connection between the elite and the mass. Insofar as the event resists being sifted through this conceptual grid, it requires us to revise that connection and is thus brought into our representation of the real by reorganizing it. Thus a suture can work, already mending in this particular area the tear between "what is happening" and "what is being thought."

At the beginning, one sign among thousands. For many it seems obvious that the events of May 1968 can be understood only through the intervention of *groupuscules,* that is, through a dangerous "elite" capable of training many of the protesters and circulating subversive ideas; an active and reflective minority alone would thus be able to account for a massive movement. This interpretation is resurgent at many points on the political or scientific horizon. It is not the fact of an interest group. And too, I would prefer not to consider whether it is accompanied by either praise or damnation of these *groupuscules.* Here I retain only a cultural "model": the idea, assumed to be an *evidence* of the mind and a *normal* procedure of comprehension, that a *mass* phenomenon is explained through the actions of an *elite*; that the crowd is by definition passive, thus ravished or victimized according to how the "leaders" want what is good for it or take their distance from it. From this one would conclude that the mass must be protected by a containing frame fashioned for its own good, and that good "directors" must be substituted for "bad" ones.

The recent events have given a better definition of this assumption because they subjected any explanation to a process of enlargement that revealed its organization. But the assumption was already dwelling in our conceptions of culture, political parties, or social structures. It commanded the implicit "philosophy" of labors that *see* in popular culture of the past nothing more than a delayed diffusion and degradation of ideas originally expressed by researchers or centers of learning.[5] This idea inspired the institution that has nonetheless worked the most for cultural promotion, but by assigning cadres to it. Since 1880, primary education has provided the structure for national cohesion and has indelibly marked French culture and society. In disseminating teaching (that is, a knowledge: what must be learned) and education (a civic morality: what must be done), has it not accelerated the destruction of local cultures? Has not cultural imperialism, which was the underside of a great social and centralizing ambition, created this "incapacity" that consists in the failure to conform to the criteria of disciplines distributed from above, intellectualized culture to the detriment of other kinds of experience, and thus impoverished local areas through what fortified centralization?[6]

The process becomes even clearer in the examinations. Here, a selection establishes scholarly itineraries on the model of a social hierarchy and filters intelligence according to the norms or mental habits of a sociocultural group. The "inept" are excluded not only from *a* culture, but also from *the* culture (since the system that eliminates them from an "instruction" also deprives them of their own traditions); and, being judged only as a function of the unique criterion imposed through the secondary school (but also through the family and through the milieu), they marginalize themselves, becoming these "self-dropouts" whom Pierre Bourdieu has studied,[7] and who, despite themselves, ultimately remain in complicity with the system that tends to perpetuate the existing relations of force.

Since then, the politics of the mass media appear to amplify — but not modify — this social conception of the relation between the elite and the public. It furnishes an immense mass with images and information manufactured in a laboratory. The organization of labor unions, political parties, or the Catholic Action Movement bears witness to an analogous structuring; it tends to turn the "base" into a receptacle of ideas or programs developed higher up, in the "centers" of thought and in the offices of the "directors."

Is it astonishing that revolutions or independence movements have been thought of in higher places only along the lines of this model, and hence as the result of an acting minority? According to this principle, it was enough to destroy the minority to suppress these movements. Many calculations or policies have been based on this cultural "evidence." It could only lead them to failure, but the social reflex is so powerful that the failure does not seem to affect it. It seems henceforth to have become — and today it is probably second nature — constitutive of a civilization of Latin and medieval origin whose oligopoly and monopoly have consolidated the endlessly leftover structure. Through a process of concentration, the modern "bourgeois" technocracy would constantly reinforce it, such that all our Western conceptions of culture would be secreting the same substance in different forms, imposing on everyone our technologies and our notorious "values" as well as our chronology and our intellectual paradigms.

Closer to home, how could the silence of the peasantry in French history be explained otherwise? How to know what were these millions of "little people," not only in the Middle Ages, but more recently, if not through what scholars and lawyers have filtered and retained? A massive unawareness consigns the "masses" to oblivion, probably because of the privilege enjoyed by written culture, because of its repression of oral culture and of *different* expressions that then became types of "folklore" along the borderlines of an empire. But this privilege belongs to scholars. It grounds the certainty, born with them and assumed by their position, that one gets to know a society as a whole by knowing what it thinks. That the learned class can change the world is the assumption of the learned class. It is also what they are doomed to *repeat* in myriad ways. A culture of teachers, professors, and readers will silence "the remainder" because it wants to be and calls itself the origin of all things. A *theoretical interpretation* is thus tied to the *power of a group* and to the structure of the society in which it conquered this position.

Without seeking sources and causes in the past, we can merely add that similar "evidence" argues for the *transmissibility* of "values" (so to speak) in a *centrifugal* way. Everything originates in the center. Everything comes down from on high. Moreover, the law that would like everything to depend on an "elite" also attaches to the transmission of culture a descending and *hierarchical* path: culture trickles down from the father to his children, from the professor to his or her students, from administrative offices to those being administrated and, in an admirable technical word, to those being "subjugated."

"The Number Began to Live"

In this framework, reality nevertheless shifted. Not long ago, Oscar Lewis remarked that, contrary to the "comfortable stereotype" according to which "it has commonly been held that peasants are a stabilizing and conservative force in human history," they have "had an important, if not crucial, role in at least four revolutions," as Pedro Martinez had shown him, because they "actively participated" in the Revolution in order to be "identified with its ideals."[8] In the American system of interpretation, this was a surprise. The words of an Aztec peasant reached back to the immense country of silent people. And for Oscar Lewis, the sociologist who hoped to let the peasant speak on his own terms, it awakened a criticism of his own North American *society* and, at the same time, it brought him to revise a *theoretical* position advanced by that society. A representation of culture was modified through this first form of a "capture of speech."

An analogous displacement is outlined in other areas, even in the arts. Thus a new theory of theater will, for example, accompany the shift that turns spectators into actors. One conception wears away whenever a theatrical (symbolic) experiment breaks the barrier between "players" and a "public," and when the latter also becomes a player by participating in a common symbolic action. But that remains an action carried out in a laboratory, or under cellophane. In a broader and less common way, this shift modifies the balance of families or universities that are "disorganized" or reorganized by the *autonomy* of "children." It affects the filiations of memory and those of patriotism. The very possibility of a "transmission" becomes problematic. What has every generation—that of the Liberation, of Algeria, and so on—taught the next generation? The relation between generations changes according to the same rhythm as the relation between contemporary cultures or nations. Something new begins to stir in history with the political independence of cultures that until now were subject to a Western intellectual grid, and even in our own country with the social autonomy of youth, which brings about the disappearance of *our* children or *our* students.

According to Philippe Ariès, since the *child* was born as a social and cultural category in the sixteenth and seventeenth centuries,[9] the *young man* could have appeared in the nineteenth century with the spread of secondary schools, the growing needs of technical training, the universalization of military service, and the beginnings of the literary figure of the "adolescent" poet. In the nineteenth century, the boy slowly withdraws from direct participation in professional structures. Apprenticeship is detached from specialized careers and is set in another time and space. But it remains a space of privilege.

Today, by overextending this space, *youth* takes on another meaning. While young people see the time of intellectual training lengthen, their irresponsibility grows along the same lines, and also (?) the game (including delinquency), the occupation of professional positions by adults hardens and emphasizes the severity of selections, a compensatory phenomenon confers on them another role: knowledge changes hands; professional training loses its prestige; permanent education becomes a collective necessity; the authority of age is devalorized. In the gap opened by the nineteenth-century adolescent, the youth of the first half of the twentieth century enters and creates an empire, but of a different order. There is a new category in the nation, and it displaces the hierarchical coordination of those that preceded it. Youth imposes itself at once on business (as a clientele of consumers) and on production (by virtue of its adaptability, etc.).[10] It suffers the nostalgic adulation of adults who then begin to depend on it. Because it carries their dreams, it formulates the demands that it can level against them. Have they not often turned it into their precious and closeted "reserve"? They themselves need this "reduction" (which, once thrust into the future, is their lost paradise), and they are afraid of it (therefore they protect their present against it). A reciprocity thus replaces "transmission" or the "integration" of the past.[11] A new organization is inaugurated. But it is not yet *recognized* for what it is. It is folded into older structures as if it were a vice, whereas in reality it invents a new structure, that is, *different* relations among categories that have changed. Rather than a rejection of the preceding generation by the following one, in terms of a conflict, mutation aims at a new type of relation between the two. It is not a rupture, but communication that is sought whenever a social and mental displacement is already written into the condition of things.

Brutal and progressive, this movement calls into question the characteristic privilege of a society and of the conception that it mirrored of "the" culture. It has irrupted in our country. It was "incomprehensible," but why? Was it because it could no longer correspond to systems of analysis built on another model? Or was it "grasped" only insofar as it was recuperated in this former model? The event thus shakes the structure of *knowledge* just as it shakes that of *society*. Clearly, it is normal that this threatened society will use its knowledge for self-defense (which also means in order to "comprehend" the crisis, but to comprehend it so that "nothing will rock the boat"). In conformity with the law of their thinking, it is normal that the "scholars" are now reducing innovation to nothing more than the repetition of their own cultural past, but devalued by its popularization, or by the action of a competing "elite." It is normal that they classify things in that way, following mental habits inhering in their "position," the massive fact that they neither wish nor are able to "know." That is all very normal. But...it is no longer true. As has been observed elsewhere, an irreducible experience has taken place. "The number began to live, to destroy, individual by individual, the myth of their abstract inertia."[12]

But would the number also have changed? Only heaven knows if the human sciences use and abuse it in the form of "quantitative" things. An indispensable instrument, thus necessary, the number perhaps still contains, beneath the methods that exclude the event and that eliminate all particularities, the argument for an "abstract inertia" of the multitude. Perhaps it is the extreme case of what allowed the cultural and technical expansionism of *one* society, but at the cost of a choice that this development implies and everywhere makes clear: the anonymity of the masses, the inertia of the number. We know that the same does not hold in other civilizations in which other types of thinking developed. At the origin of a science, there are always ethical and cultural options. Today, the historical and social a prioris of our knowledge are best revealed through the event itself.[13]

Not that one "piece of evidence" *needs* to be replaced by another. It is a matter of a critical question. No longer can we assume evidence to be what had been so up to now. Experiences have changed our assurance; no theory can escape that fact. Every human science has to introduce doubt into its own development in order to investigate where it stands in its historical relation to a social type. It has a stake in *one* form of culture. In order to redefine itself, it has to proceed to an analysis that challenges the civilization for which it argues.

Between a society and its scientific models, between a historical situation and the intellectual tools that belong to it, there exists a relation that constitutes a cultural system. The event can change it, thus calling for the readjustment of cultural representations and social institutions. In knowledge, it will be translated *either* by a refusal—but so too the new and concealed role hereafter assigned to conceptions that have become archaic—*or* by a displacement that is explained by the appearance of theories corresponding to a different cultural experience. Seen from this angle, and from this angle alone, Herbert Marcuse's writings can help us to state this problem precisely, for they assemble under the rubric of a single problematic the development of our civilization and that of the so-called human sciences.

The Function of Knowledge in Consumer Society (Herbert Marcuse)

Marcuse seems to have retained from his revolutionary past the taste for concepts sculpted like bricks.[14] His intellectual instruments are unwieldy but because they would like to be pervasively engaging. He reads like a news writer for *Time* magazine, probably because he wants to make his model visible. In his view, our society has become so victimized by the law of "profit" that any opposition—political, social, or religious—is assimilated into the system and can offer hardly a trace, other than some "ideological" leftovers, of the resistance needed for a social dynamism. One wants to refer to—or believes one still is referring to—*another* dimension of humanity; but, in reality, it is eliminated by the development of civilization that catches every activity in the tightly knit web of production and consumption. In Heideggerian terms (that do not belong to Marcuse), we might say that the thinking that counts, that calculates, and that is infinitely absorbed by its productive operation causes meditation, a mode of reflection that "is in pursuit of meaning that dominates in everything that is," to vanish or be forgotten.[15] For Marcuse, this "meditating" reflection is contestatory, essential to people who refuse to be reduced to instruments of labor or commodities of commercialization. But this refusal can only be a fiction.

In fact, a social logic unwittingly displaces primitively autonomous sectors and sets them under its purview, but without their theory accounting for this tacit functioning. Thus social demands are turned into sources of *profit* (the enrichment of poorer classes assuring sales to a clientele); spiritual protests into therapies *useful* to the establishment (an "adaptation" endlessly adjusts ideals to "reality" and thus suppresses the interrogative resistance of an absolute); "negative" thinking, the symptom of an irreducible alterity, into a functionalism that metamorphoses the intellectual and social criterion of rational "operations" into things "operative" and hence *efficacious* (the way in which general interests direct private research toward what can be commercialized).

Thus the oppositions that drew their origin from a needed contestation begin, slowly, with an often static doctrine, to play a role contrary to what they had announced. They fly under a new flag but are conscripted into the service of an anonymous necessity. They are effectively put to uses other than what their theory dictates. They become *ideologies* that deceive, that are satisfied with offering to liberty an alibi that masks their real docility with respect to a "capitalism" that has become, in the words of Max Weber, "a system of slavery without a master."

This form of discrete "repression" organized by American civilization corresponds to a present situation. It is historical in nature. It would be built over a more structural repression of a psychosocial type: the "pleasure principle" is always repressed by society. "Our civilization is founded on the repression of instincts." Thus Marcuse takes up Freud's words. But these *repressed* instincts are also, through a "return of the repressed," *represented* in the language that censors them. Individual and collective lapses alike, dysfunctionings and traces of every kind, allow this endlessly leftover and masked "repressed" to appear in the very expressions of repression. Marcuse's thinking can thus certainly be broadened.

From time to time, a volcanic rift opens up a submerged violence with an abrupt explosion of language. A verbal lava, already metamorphosed in its irruption into daylight, attests to what repression has done to the repressed; for if human history is the history of repression, "the return of what was repressed" nonetheless constitutes a permanently dangerous underground, a secret and resurgent life in every civilization that takes the form of an instinct forever obliterated by law but that always threatens. A revolution would be simmering beneath the feet of every society, as witnessed by the very repetition of its failures. Every piece of speech would signify the violence of an irrepressible *desire*, but in the social language that represses and "betrays" it (in the double sense of the term: to deceive and to reveal) with *needs* to satisfy or that are satisfied.

Thus, two kinds of "repression" are collapsed into one. The former is inherent in all societies, and the latter characterizes a present situation. Marcuse designates the latter as "surrepression" and esteems it to be a repetition of the first. This architecture attempts to superimpose the one on the other, that is, both the historical (in economy) and the structural (in psychology).

Now we have to take leave of Marcuse if we want to seriously consider the dilemma that he is positing; for right where he believes he is speaking of (economic and psychological) *realities* for the sake of demonstrating the new conflation, he is really confronting the two great *systems of interpretation* to which each are referred in order to understand what is happening: Marxism and Freudianism. These systems both date from the second half of the nineteenth century and the first half of the twentieth century. They are themselves inscribed in history. Now, in analyzing the recent development of society, Marcuse shows a displacement not only in the "ideologies" he examines but in the sciences to which he makes reference. In his work, a crossfire is produced in which the role that was originally given to each is inverted. Marxism, the theoretical instrument of a revolution based on the critical examination of relations of production, becomes a force deployed by the consumer society. Inversely, Freudianism, which was passed off as a method facilitating or restoring the integration of individuals into society, becomes sign of the irreducibility of whatever the "pleasure principle" constitutes as something left over or repressed.

Marcuse is led to draw this chiasm by using two currently cardinal "human sciences" simply because he wants to analyze the "monstrous" development of American consumer society. He is unable to account for *what civilization has become* unless his demonstration also involves *what these two sciences have become*. Described as the emergence of a new social system, a history (or a becoming) is legible in the reployment of the two scientific systems, that is, in the distance that separates their current functioning from their primitive use. Knowledge and society simultaneously "budge."

What Marcuse *does with* these sciences (when he wants to describe this global evolution on his own account) he also *states*, but only obliquely. He notes the displacement of social categories on which these sciences had founded a type of investigation: for Marxism, the creative and revolutionary role of *labor*; in Freudianism, the repressive and dominating function of the *father*. In his view, labor ceased to be creative once it was integrated into the system of production; furthermore, it is especially hard labor, pain and fatigue, whose compensation is the alienated liberty of leisure. In this configuration, as a social figure the father vanishes in order to be replaced by the anonymity of a society whose law becomes more imposing in that no single character can figure at the head of collective revolt.

No matter how inexact Marcusian analysis may be, the procedure it follows and the theoretical questions it raises are capital: on the one hand, the *method* that makes possible the examination of civilization consists in exhuming the *social* assumptions of psychoanalysis (the role of the father being linked to a type of civilization), at the same time that it takes up Marxian categories in the name of *psychological* structures of society (labor being inscribed in a more fundamental repression). In other words, Marcuse exceeds the framework of "specializations" — or a former classification of the sciences — in order to grasp the global extent of a new system. But if it is true that consideration of a different *totality* is formulated with the reciprocal critique of the sciences developed in the context of another time, what instrument do we have to analyze our own time? It seems that a new stage of civilization can be grasped only along a fault line (in this space that is the residual trace of the movement of intellectual constellations), or rather through the crisscrossing of sciences proportioned to a moment in the past.

That too is the *theoretical question* opened by *Eros and Civilization* and *One Dimensional Man,* if we admit — as these two works aim to prove — that "class conflict" (determined by the relations of labor in capitalism) and rivalry with the father (in a strongly hierarchized family and social structure) tend to become concepts inadequate to the real. Although he rejects the easy category of a "culturalism" that is really only a sloppy empiricism, Marcuse offers us the spectacle of a new social logic that corresponds only to a disarmed logic.[16] He says as much (perhaps more than he would wish) through the type of conflation he makes between Marxism and Freudianism: in order to revise and coordinate the instruments at his disposal, in order to adjust them to the reality he wishes to take account of, he nails them together in an unconvincing intellectual carpentry.

For example, he wants to determine *where* a resistance can be found that might invigorate humans in industrial society with a second "dimension." He has to find *somewhere* a truth or an innocence in which a society of happiness can be born. In that way he might even further resemble his two masters. Freud scoured history in muttering to himself, "There's got to be a cadaver somewhere or other!" But for him everything was the sign of something missing, of the murdered father. Marx, for his part, everywhere discerned an organizing force of society, the birth of the proletariat. Marcuse flaccidly mimicks both of them. He attaches an identical role to the opposition that is born with the social outcasts and to the one that is always resurgent with the return of repressed pleasure: the lumpen proletariat and art share a similar function of "rejection" in respect to the one-dimensional universe. The idea is interesting. It is adjusted to the fact that the alliance to which social unrest now attests associates misery and poetry. Like a label, the idea designates the fact rather than its analysis. It too hastily marries a shard of Marxism to a shard of Freudianism in order to force both to say that "truth" or salvation are found in the same place.

To be sure, these two systems share this resemblance of being geologies that explain the configuration of the earth by its relation to fundamental infrastructures. But in this relation they are not placing "reality" in the same spot. The former locates it somewhere in the economic infrastructure; the latter refuses to establish a site for it, or rather keeps it as something endlessly both represented *and* lost in the reciprocal relation of resistance and repression. By crossing the two, Marcuse constructs hybrid concepts with notions that are elaborated as functions of different analytical procedures. Furthermore, he assigns them the role of plugging up the same hole, of filling the lacuna of a "second dimension."

For him, it is enough to know if indeed, yes or no, social "truth" has a place; if human destinies can be localized; and, as a consequence, if the resistance or the "great refusal" somewhere owns a principle on which the future would depend. He *wants* to point his finger at the axis of a future revolution, and he *knows* that it cannot be what Marxism had indicated. He thus explains through a Freudian analysis of social repression the failure of "Marxist" revolutions, and he buys into an instinctual liberation, the source of an "erotic" accomplishment of man in nature, the Marxist dream of a classless society.

When, with his weapons and his intellectual baggage, he passes from the Marxist to the Freudian revolution, he keeps from the first the "model" of a topography of the opposition and perhaps finds in the second what he needs to justify his disillusionment or his skepticism.[17] What, in the guise of a Marxist, he had considered as the site of the revolution and the force of history from an economic and social perspective—the proletariat—he then retains as a place hereafter "co-opted" and integrated into the civilization of the present day; but he conserves the idea of somewhere nailing down the resistance whose failure Freudianism will allow him to explain. His reading of Freud remains staunchly Marxist insofar as it unduly transposes onto the field of psychoanalysis a cast of roles or forces that had meaning only in economy or sociology. His work takes on the fascinating but partially deceptive allure of a tragic epic.

It is an *Iliad*. The epic portrays a war of the gods, the struggle of Eros and Thanatos, of the "pleasure instinct" and of the "profit principle," and other abstractions. A lucid revolutionary who is increasingly disillusioned. In this respect, *One Dimensional Man* marks a clear withdrawal in relation to the (purely "prophetic") optimism of *Eros and Civilization*, a work that opened the hypothesis of a liberation as a sort of deus ex machina. But his thinking has continued to vacillate between a miracle to come — that he would renounce only in ceasing to be himself — and the totalitarian *functioning* whose new and repressive character he analyzes. A resident of La Jolla, as if on an Olympus over San Diego that dominates opposing superpowers, he follows their endless battles. Victory no longer goes from one side to the other and could never be final. In truth, identified with the "poor" or with artists, David is always slain by Goliath. His revolt, by protesting a repressed truth, emits only sterile and impoverished words.

But at least Marcuse has the courage — which prompts "specialists" to smile — to put society at large on trial.[18] That is the genre of his essay, in which he proportions a *method* to the *object* of the examination, since his study of the possibility of revolution in the current system is tied to an attempt to overcome the compartmentalization of the human sciences. In that way, he shows — and the point is fundamental — that a shift reaches both social divisions and scientific classifications; that it concerns a praxis and its theory; and that, finally, it can be *lived* only if it can be *thought* in the wake of a shift in thinking. He also carries out his analysis in a way that *designates* (or symbolizes) a *global* problem, but without being able to give it an adequate conceptual apparatus. May less whoever can do better cast the first stone! Through this double aspect of his work, Marcuse indicates a task to be done. He also connects to the questions opened up since May 1968, even if we were to assume that on the topic of Marcuse the words of Talleyrand after the fall of Villèle could be recalled: he leaves behind an emptiness that is greater than the place he occupied.

Social Structures and Systems of Representation

A putative grandfather of the "extremists" of Nanterre (which in fact is not true), Marcuse conflates two current types of interrogation on the future and on the meaning of our society. With him we can be led to think that they are indissociable and, by extracting them from his work, we can bind them in the following way.

1. A same contestatory opposition is offered in two different forms (at least according to the former classifications) that have in common being the effects of a sociocultural repression: the one, "bourgeois," of an intelligentsia (frustrated by the benefits it expected from university privileges, or lucid about the nature of the "service" that society asks of it); the other, "proletarian," of the socially excluded, the culturally homeless — foreigners, subcultures of "paupers," the lumpen proletariat, and so on. Here is the beginning of a *social reorganization* if a *same* force were able to be constituted from places that, today, social organization is *separating*.

2. At stake also is a *reorganization of the human sciences.* Born of a history (that of the nineteenth and early twentieth centuries), Marxist economy and Freudian psychology were displaced by later events, but this slippage has not yet received the theoretical status of another taxonomy of sciences; it intervenes only surreptitiously, in the name of their new functioning. The order of reason already obeys a law that continues to escape it. But it must represent it through its own reorganization. The objects defined and labeled by sciences born only yesterday (the "proletariat," for example, or the "unconscious") corresponded to methods of investigation; they cannot be taken as immutable realities; they are linked to the scientific organization that had to produce reason and permit the analysis of *a* human situation. A past is invested in a scientific theory and in its "objects." A more recent history thus appeals to a new structuration for the categories of knowledge, and in that way it will gain meaning.

We find these two aspects of cultural change expressed during the crisis of May 1968 in the form of an interrogation (but one that remained marginal to the system that was brought back to reality by the resurgence in June). This is not surprising, since the protests were dealing with an *organization* of society *and* of its representations. A few examples demonstrate that the questioning of *"order"* was a throwback to the mutation of a *reason.*

1. The association of "bourgeois" students and the "sleaze" is only one indication of a much more basic attempt to *overcome,* as "laborers," the *division* between workers and students. A division was becoming archaic because of a movement that had already arisen; but the fact was not yet recognized by conceptual modes and theories that shouldered the weight of their historical origins. It was translated only by what students and workers had *become,* and by the homologous lag of conceptions that were supposed to "represent" them.

A revision of structures is also implied by the movement that now envisions culture in the name of a solidarity with "excluded" groups. It wishes to overcome a classification and thus shift a type of organization. The demarcation itself becomes the "tactical" site of a *global* revision. Thus Pierre Bourdieu and Jean-Claude Passeron begin with the "eliminated" in order to study schooling or national examinations[19]—not that those who are eliminated can themselves define what true culture must be (as if "truth" were in their hands)! But the problem of a culture that could be everyone's language is posed beyond the divisions that are assumed by a demarcation based on social criteria. In the same way, many works contest a *general* division of civilization when they *reject the boundary* created through the isolation of a "workers'" culture, of a "poor France," or of "another America."[20] Even if their authors merely become the explorers of an "other" region, they must not be interpreted as if one side had to gain preference over the other. In fact, their studies challenge the dividing line, and in that way they call into question a sociocultural system. Everywhere "contestation is 'negative' insofar as it is outside of the divisions and the disciplines of established society."[21]

2. The revision of the compartmentalization between disciplines is also part of a structural shift. The theoretical status of each discipline holds less to the definition that it ascribes to itself than to its relation with others, that is, its inscription in a network of reciprocal determinations.[22] A renewal is therefore not possible if one is pigeonholed inside of a (or each) discipline: one thus necessarily confirms the system that is implied by its specific place in the constellation of an epistemological classification—or, in the more immediate sense, in the organization of this universe of knowledge called the "university." Structural innovation takes place only in interdisciplinarity, wherever *relations* can be grasped and debated, wherever boundaries and significant divisions of a system can be challenged.

In a "savage" form, such were the discussions and the procedures of the educational reforms of May 1968. For example, the relation between general assemblies and commissions showed how, simultaneously, social groups and divisions of disciplines were being shifted. The role of the assembly as a witness to a certain "universality" consisted less in developing projects than criticizing situations put forward through the work of a commission and in explaining its theoretical consequences for the sake of structuring. In a sense, this criticism unveiled in a *discipline* its relation with a historical *situation*.

It made possible a revision of knowledge through the clarification of an axiomatic datum: relations among sciences and a position vis-à-vis students were implied through the very localization of a reformist project. A discipline needed to be examined from a global point of view, in a general assembly, in order for its unspoken function or its forgotten history to be brought into view and then modified.

In other words, a *theoretical* revision of disciplines could only call into question the connections that held them together and reveal an entire system of historical and social relations — which also amounts to a combination of places occupied and of powers held. Inversely, the specific *action* of students to get out of their isolation (which they saw as an encirclement, or a "ghetto") and to demonstrate their solidarity with the workers could not fail to be related to the structures of thought that were defining the relation of the elite to the masses or the transmission of knowledge (by fathers, priests, or directors) — a thought that was located in the apparatus of the "opposition" merely replacing a hierarchy of a party with a hierarchy of classes (contrary forces or doctrines are ultimately indifferent; they are reciprocally devoted to homologous mental organizations through the sole force of the system that holds them together).

In the first case, a theoretical discussion referred to a conflation of powers; in the second, a praxis contradicted a "division" (what is known as a division of sciences) and appealed to another conceptualization, one that might provide the category of "workers" with a determining role in a different social combination.

The effect and the meaning of a crisis are revealed in the connections and latent cohesions, especially because a profound shift makes them evident only when they are uprooted. Can one, from that point, splinter the problem and redivide it into questions proportioned to the compartments that an order constituted — or a social reason — that has since been displaced? That is the option of a narrow reformism. It wishes to account for a *global* shift only inside of the division or as a function of categories that are specifically linked to the social architecture in question. In that way, it censures the question itself. It refuses it. It has an excuse or a justification that is also a fact: the "poverty" of concepts or actions that attempted to signify a modification of the entire system. People conclude with assurance that it is nothing more than a psychodrama or an outlet, and that we have to be "realistic," that is, reform each sector in isolation so as to respond to each of the ills bandied about by the rhetoric of a few commonplaces. This conclusion is hastily drawn and, I believe, erroneous, as would be one that challenged the question posed by Marcuse by arguing that he had not produced a theory of his vision.

In an established order, every deeper movement can be *symbolized* only through a different use of methods or conceptions developed as a function of procedures that are themselves epistemologically linked to earlier constructions of knowledge. This new use is thus *incorrect* with respect to past definitions, and *imprecise* with respect to determinations that would make another organization possible. Understood in this way, the symbol is a joke. It amuses, it irritates specialists or directors who sit in worlds of the past that can now be exploited. They may be right about novelties. Despite the myriad emergence of its symptoms, every beginning is fragile, and no necessity will mirror it in order to assure its success. The inheritors of established forms of knowledge are not, however, correct. The shifts are running through their own disciplines; they are already perceptible in the distortions of their system, in the same way that their own concepts are being recaptured by protesting groups.

A myopic politics is one that refuses what is translated *both* by these distortions in the inner function and by outer irruptions that still lack new and "correct" definitions. It is aimed at preparing museums, not a society. More audacious and, ultimately, more lucid in matters of knowledge, is the politics that discerns in the diversity of signs the symbol of a general movement and thus the indication of a reorganization that needs to be undertaken. But, whereas intellectual courage no more suffices than does lucidity alone, here a choice is needed, one linked to the ambition of beginning over again, that is, of living.

Chapter 8
Culture within Society

Stripped of the data and the details that ought to flesh out this study, this chapter presents a sketch that is intentionally skeletal. The notes that follow simply intend to clarify a few prerequisites and explain a few choices. The position being taken here applies the results of some practical analyses to a few social and political options. Clearly, we cannot assume that somewhere a dominant point of view can be found that can help us study the present and the future of a society. With respect to global or prospective vantage points, the observation of what took place, or of what in fact is happening, everywhere brings forth a double crisis, of programming and of theoretical instrumentalization. The disappearance of universal principles is one aspect of the current situation. Since our theoretical models hardly allow us to think of embedded or sedimented systems in plural ways, we must first of all recognize — even if by trial and error — how modes of reasoning that were once necessary can spring out of particular situations and be put to new tasks.

ABCs of Culture

The growing importance of cultural problems is framed in a broad context. This context is characterized first of all by the logic of a society, based on production, that has responded to the elementary needs of the population that pays for them and that, in order to expand, must analyze, develop, and satisfy some of its users' "cultural" needs. Thus psychoanalysis is a source of profit for advertisers; psychology is worth being invested in the organization of corporate enterprises; in the industrial sector, the production of dictionaries, records, or gadgets both supplements and replaces traditionally man-ufactured goods.

Added to that is the ineptness of economic plans or actions that could respond directly to the harmful effects that, beyond a given threshold, are engendered by progress itself (pollution, drugs, environmental degradation, and so on; and the great collective illnesses of which these phenomena are symptoms, characteristic of humans living "at the edge of saturation").[1] Finally, one must also underscore the absence of fundamental criteria that might enlighten the predictions or reorientations that are now needed for a system increasingly proportioned to "people who only want to have something" and decreasingly to those who "want to be somebody."[2]

Today, rather than a sum of "values" that need to be defended or of ideas to be promoted, culture connotes a labor to be undertaken over the entire expanse of social life. In this way, a prerequisite operation is needed to locate in the rich flow of culture a social functioning, a topography of questions or a topic, a field of strategic possibilities and of political implications.

The questions, organizations, and actions that are assumed to be cultural represent both symptoms and responses with respect to structural changes in society. The interpretation of these signs—whose species is proliferating—initially refers to their *social functioning*.

As soon as an operation is envisaged, the rifts must be sought through which the process develops, allowing for a formulation of the problems. The study of information concerning culture is conditioned by this topography of questions or "topic."

Then another stage intervenes, that of choices. Objectives need to be specified as a function of the analysis of given situations. A few sites where criteria can be defined need to be mapped out in places where interventions can truly correct or modify current processes. Thus is obtained *a field of strategic possibilities*.

The decisions designated by a strategy call into question an organization of powers. To make this relation clear is tantamount to returning to the social system through *a political analysis*.

Every report that deals with cultural problems moves on a ground of unstable words. It is impossible to impose any conceptual definition on these terms. Their meanings are tied to functions in disparate ideologies and systems. At the very least, a meaning must be assigned to the use that will be made here of *culture* and *cultural*.

The term *culture* intervenes in the "diffusion of culture," "popular culture," "politics of culture," and so on. Six different uses — characterized by as many different approaches — can be designated:

1. The features of "cultivated" human beings, that is, corresponding to the model developed in stratified societies through a category that introduces its norms wherever it imposes its power.
2. A patrimony of "works" to be preserved or diffused, or in relation to which to be situated (for example, classical culture, humanistic culture, Italian culture, English culture, etc.). Added to the idea of "works" to be disseminated is that of "creations" and "creators" to be privileged in view of a renewal of a given patrimony.
3. The image, perception, or comprehension of a world belonging to a given milieu (rural, urban, Indian, etc.) or to a time (medieval, contemporary, etc.): Max Weber's *Weltanschauung*, A. O. Lovejoy's *Unit Idea*, and so on. To this conception, which ascribes to its tacit "ideas" the role of organizing experience, can be compared André Malraux's social aesthetics, a substitute for philosophical or religious visions of the world.
4. Modes of behavior, institutions, ideologies, and myths that compose frames of reference and whose totality, whether it is coherent or not, distinguishes one society from another. Since E. B. Tylor's *Primitive Culture* (1871), it has become a key concept in cultural anthropology (cf. "patterns of culture"). An entire spectrum of positions exists whereby one privileges practices and behaviors or ideologies and myths.
5. Things acquired, insofar as they are distinguished from things innate. Culture leans in the direction of creation, artifice, and operativity in a dialectic that is opposed to it and combines it with nature.
6. A system of communication, conceived according to models developed in theories of verbal language. Especially underscored are the rules that organize the passage of signifiers or, in a related field, media (cf. A. Moles). Here the meaning of 4 above must be retained to determine a level

of analysis with the goal of specifying a way of taking up the problem.

Subculture and *counterculture* need to be distinguished. The former designates the culture of a subgroup, of a minority, and so on. The latter refers to the judgment that a majority makes of subcultures or subgroups and whose social implications the subgroups often confirm when they take them up in order to define themselves.[3]

Cultural appears in a series of frequently used expressions: "cultural action," "cultural activity," "cultural affairs," "cultural agents," "cultural center," "cultural chain," "cultural discourse," "cultural development," "cultural foyer," "cultural engineer," "cultural leisures," "cultural politics," "cultural revolution," "cultural system," "cultural life," and so on. Out of this almost endless list a few themes emerge.

Cultural action, an expression parallel to "union action" or "political action," designates an intervention linking the agents to specific goals (or "targets"). It is also an operational segment in which the means of mobilizing a project are more important than the goals to be defined.

Cultural activity locates activity in an inherited and patented culture (cf. meanings 1 and 2 of *culture* above), that is, in "cultivated culture" (Edgar Morin).

Cultural agents mean those who exercise one of the functions or one of the positions defined by the cultural field: creator, animator, critic, disseminator, consumer, and so on.

Cultural politics could be considered the more or less coherent totality of objectives, means, and actions aiming at modifying behavior according to explicit principles or criteria.

Cultural discourse can be understood as all language that deals with cultural problems insofar as a relation exists between a form and a content.

Cultural development submits to the law of a homogeneous growth the reforms needed for an extension of production or consumption. An ideology of continuity and, in particular, of the invariability of the socioeconomic system upholds the concept of *development* and opposes it to those of "cultural revolution" or "structural" changes.

As a result, the concept of "development" extends its power to mobilize, but only as cultural problems are introduced and reclassified in the sphere of long-range planning. A triple revolution accompanies this technocratic reclassification:

1. *Thematics* progressively ceases to appeal to a social origin and norm in order to concentrate on the idea of a present that needs to be managed and a future that has to be controlled.
2. *Institutions* that were formerly private and militant are increasingly drawn into structures of state and into an administration of long-term planning.
3. *Objectives* that initially aimed at revising social equilibrium turn in the direction of the organization of techniques, organisms, and professions (that raise consciousness, cultural engineers, etc.) endowed with an instrumental value with the aim of facilitating participation in a politics defined elsewhere, in high places.

A Social Functioning

For the sake of an approximate picture we must ask how the ingredients that produce the amalgam, generally qualified today in the name of "culture," *can be described*. A few elements emerge from ongoing analyses.

1. The Valorization of Knowledge

The scientific and technical rationalization of European societies progressively diminishes the value and the profitability of the labor of direct production. It replaces and marginalizes labor through automation. It redirects the mass of human works toward preparation, organization, or the control of production. It privileges knowledge.[4]

Little by little, a new category of technicians—adjoined to automated machinery—replaces an ever-growing amount of unskilled labor that for its own development industrial society had for more than a century relegated to factories. An "economy of human resources" follows from this quantitative mobilization. It requires "investments in human beings," but when they are rationalized, these investments are achieved according to the principles of a selection that favors those who are best placed according to criteria of age (young), place (new cities), and social status (the "new petite bourgeoisie").

2. A Restructuring of Private Life in Relation to Professional Life

In European nations, which in many respects are still traditional societies, the adaptations to technical requirements of labor leave intact or brutally cut through—even if superficially—the deeper structures of affective life and personal frames of reference.

The need to create new styles of life is not only tied to the delays caused by private life on professional life, but to a specifically Western tension: everyday life runs directly against the grain of a collective conviction that has been a typically Western structure for more than four centuries, namely, that a connection must exist between productive labor and personal development. This idea is foreign to ancient or medieval societies (such as Japanese society, it appears), in which personal achievement is located in areas other than labor.

Now, as a greater distance develops in professional life with regard to labor (in play, cynicism, or boredom), in private life opaque resistances get rooted in investments left intact. This tension is especially felt in nations whose space tends to be more closed, whose history is longer, and whose coherence is stronger.

The need to find a space, to be resituated in relation to institutions of private life (family, marriage, household, locality), to list the forms of achievement on the basis of risk, to explore other *styles of life*: this is a source of debates, research, and reactions that are now composing a cultural expression. Ultimately, these are forms of life that intensive research is currently testing and documenting.

3. The Society of Spectacle

Because the ability to produce is really organized around rationales or economic powers, collective representations turn into objects of folklore. Ideological instances are transformed into spectacles. Risk and creativity are excluded from festivals (at least the daily double maintains some risk). Legends for seated spectators proliferate in the space of leisure made possible by and necessary for a downscaled and "constrained" labor. By contrast, the possibilities of action accumulate wherever financial means and technical competence are concentrated. In this regard, "cultural" growth is symptomatic of the movement that tranforms the "people" into a "public."[5]

Does this spell the end of militant movements? Surviving the demystification of ideologies are, nonetheless, some militants without causes. They are often found in the places where new myths are being constructed: for example, in new cities constituted as exceptional places, in the signs of newly found coherence, in the paradise of a social truth. Two social types thus cooperate in the edification of these symbolic points of reference where spectacle and production are linked: militants converted into cultural agents, and planners who have become "cultural engineers."

4. A Neuter Form: The Cultural

In language, "culture" has a neuter inflection. It is the symptom of the existence of a backwater into which flow all the problems that a society, unable to assimilate otherwise, leaves aside. They are left in these currents, isolated from their structural ties with the appearance of new powers and displacements emerging from social conflict or from local economic developments. Culture happens to be assumed as something indistinct and soft. It is characterized as a nonplace in which everything goes, in which "anything" can circulate.

When it is not enclosed in statistics and the analytical detail of data, cultural discourse falls into generalities and recycles doctrinal residues of politics, philosophy, and religion. This universal discourse is the museum in which a few concepts, extracted from systems that formerly had enjoyed a certain rigor ("humanism," etc.), are pigeonholed. Thus ideology is surreptitiously resurgent in things cultural — a handiwork of ideology, an ideological grab bag, that probably is the sign of something else to come.

So-called cultural politics is itself often the victim of this neuter or neutral form — despite the studies and the critical apparatus at its disposal — when, for the purpose of treating it elsewhere, it marks off an abstract cultural "dimension" in the organization of society.[6] It is a strange "politics" because its political problems are wiped away. The politics performs "as if" (furthermore, we know this to be a fiction) the global price to be paid could be avoided when a change is enacted in any given sector of society.

A Topography of Questions

Among many others, three ruptures appear especially significant, even if their gravity varies according to their region. They are not reducible to effects of deterioration in the system. Rather, they are symptomatic of a transmission between something that is ending and something that is beginning.

1. Institutions and Initiatives

Public institutions that can bear the label of "culture" in France (not only the administration of museums or theaters, etc., but especially National Education, national television, etc.) have gotten flabby by increasing their volume. Unable to control the forces that are folded into them and that control them without having to be named as such, these great bodies are nonetheless unable to regulate, articulate, or merely "assist" initiatives that are swarming just beneath or in the margins, and for which quite often personal relations have a lot to say. The science of action is developed in laboratories, at a considerable remove from that reality.

In themselves, institutions obey the rule of a two-sided game. If their facade is that of public organizations, the power that inhabits them belongs to social groups established in the name of owners of innovation and to trusts that monopolize their means. The consequence of this internal division is in the marginal development of countercultures, swimming along the edges of each structure (education, press, theater, etc.): a swarming just under the surface, a multifarious life corresponds to what official legend calls the *underground*. How could a regulation be coordinated between public organizations colonized through interest groups and this renewal of private initiatives?

This situation is a sign at once of the existence of a creativity and the nature of cultural institutions in a country traditionally attached to acquired situations and paralyzed by bureaucracies. Innovation clearly comes about, but in a catch-as-catch-can way, or in the shadows where originality is allowed. Public organizations remain in place, and even extend themselves; but they are trapped in their victory over change, impoverished by the exile or repression of any real opposition, and deprived not of powers, but of powers that might be their own.

The rejection of initiatives toward marginalization ultimately attests to an eradication of diversity. What is lost in this fashion, what is eliminated from public view, is what has until now always inspired and fertilized the cultural and biological life of human societies: qualitative differences. Conformism triumphs with the quantitative development held by the same groups. Its success camouflages inner oppositions; it only allows heterogeneous things to surge forth surreptitiously. A condition of social existence thus seems to be lacking.

2. Culture and Passivity

Planted in leisure activities where it plays a compensatory role for labor, consumer culture massively develops among its spectators a passivity of which it is already its own effect. It represents the sector where the movement that reduces the number of actors and increases that of *passive* subjects is accelerating most rapidly in the nation.

It seems that the more time *allocated* to leisure activities increases (which represents progress), the less leisure is something that is *chosen*. Information especially (the press, television, video, etc.) reserves to a smaller and smaller circle of producers the possession or use of increasingly expensive equipment. Instruction tends to practice social selection through the path of a hierarchization that orders intellectual levels according to the powers of groups or of classes: thus the upper echelon creates a widening gap between elite schools, universities, and technical schools.[7] The financing of sports goes to competition more than to public education. Despite all that is being said, the cultural centers really serve only the privileged layers of society and culture. Many attempts or partial reforms do not succeed in changing the logic of a system. Budgetary choices and promotional programs are really what favor the Malthusian growth of creation.

This situation mixes in the totality of the nation a diminution of creators with a multiplication of consumers. A new partitioning of language corresponds to the phenomenon. Where professional, political, religious, regional, and other groups had once organized their convictions into discourses representative of affective investments and collective convictions, the demystification of ideologies causes a redistribution of languages according to their degree of effectiveness or operativity.

Reserved for an elite is a technical or scientific language that is endowed with a transformative power. It remains foreign to the general population to which it is offered, through popularization, as something incomprehensible. Another, specular, language takes pride in expressing and presenting to an entire society a mirror addressed to everyone and ultimately reflective of no one. It is pure decoration. These two regimes of culture are no longer differentiated by "values," by contents, by their "quality," or by the special interests of groups. They are distinguished by their relation to action. Here is where culture is divided and reorganized—its least operative part becoming by far the most extensive.

Thus also creation is what is shown but never proposed. Communication, violence, power relations, love, and eroticism—ultimately all forms of "human" intervention—are the stuff of consumer literature, but only because they are lacking in practical experience. Language makes a spectacle of the actions that a society no longer allows. What subjects lose is sold back to them in the form of commodities to be consumed.

3. Economic Production and Communication

In its past usage, "commerce" designated the exchange of people more than the trafficking or negotiation of things. The current restriction of this word to a "commercial" inflection can be considered to be the symptom of an entire evolution. Exchanges are now measured in terms of economic relations. They ultimately conform to the law of a productivist society that is now capable of creating a sum of goods to be consumed (products) and, among eventual buyers, corresponding "needs" to be met (advertising). In an industrial society, reference to natural needs is the protective myth of campaigns determined by the logic of the marketplace, campaigns that encounter needs only as forms of resistance or limits.

From that point on, can the cultural contents determined by these exchanges and mobilized along the pathways of the media ever be taken seriously? They have nothing to say about the forces that really organize them. They are infected by an ambiguity that makes them entirely insignificant (in the way that literary analysis barely draws attention to content in favor of formal problems of structural organization). Ultimately, any discourse can be used since the system that subtends contents directs them wherever it wishes. Freedom of speech can be great where words and images are afloat without specifying the currents that buoy and carry them. Conservative or revolutionary ideologies, a whole array of characters (Marx, Freud, Astérix, Dr. Joyce Brothers, Ruth Westheimer, etc.), go through the same channels. They all look alike and are inoffensive because they all play together in the same "theater" where real (economic) exchanges begin behind the curtains.

As a result, enterprises, administrations, and the media powers set off in quest of values and seek to restore human relations. But language cannot be invested seriously by means of values manufactured from the recycled scraps of the past or of religion, thanks to legends—the philosophy of the poor—that speak of participation, nor even by exploiting the resources of social psychology in order to reinforce the system by sealing off the yawning gaps of the relation. Reciprocally, communication becomes an obsession in social practice. Wherever they can, the press and the radio deceive or satisfy this "solitary crowd" with celestial magic, the exoticism of easy love, or the terrors of drugs. What spreads is the feeling of a fatality. Humans are *spoken* by the language of socioeconomic determinism long before they can speak it. What is the use of all these words, since they can no longer be believed because they neither open closed doors nor change things? Only comedy or enigmas remain. Paradoxically, a renewal of mythologies accompanies the technical progress of production.

Will it be possible for humans to create spaces for themselves in which their own speech can be proffered? Can criteria of action be built on economic exchanges and on one another? Will it be possible to be located somewhere as being different in relation to others, at a time when information and social participation are every day crushing the effects of difference?[8]

A Field of Strategic Possibilities

How can a regulation of initiatives be organized, cultural expression reconciled with a constructive activity, and human communication united with economic production? These questions refer not only to obvious facts, but to divisions that organize the growth of "culture." Furthermore, in their totality they describe the effects of a general situation of which the isolation of the "cultural" is merely one indication. As soon as they are established in a form of their own in relation to social, economic, and political problems, cultural affairs bring about, in each of their sectors, the rift that causes them to develop the way they do. If we accept this fictive autonomy as an analytical given, the tendency of "culture" to become a political alibi will be emphasized, and it will form an inert weight in the social body.

Once this scheme is established with a goal of accounting for deficits, it becomes possible to project a few options. In order to resolve the visible tensions, in order to promote cultural development without aggravating its isolation, a strategy will aim at locating points that allow for concrete and significant intervention. It can only be based on ongoing experiences, alone capable of opening possibilities, but it must combine them in a "field" according to criteria that base decisions to be taken in the face of a proliferation of projects and initiatives.

1. Sociocultural Units Taking Shape

Two of these strategic points seem to me to be especially important.

Alienation is currently linked to cultural isolation. Social movements have precisely had as their goal and their effect to break the vicious circle of culture and reveal the established powers that it conceals. They make clear or restore the relations of cultural situations (of the worker, the female, young people, vacationers, etc.) with the type of social relations maintained by economic systems.

Another observation: current forms of consciousness-raising make clear at the same time the transformation of political or union organizations that until now represented the interests and the convictions of collective groups. They work in a different way, either because their clientele is fragmented and partially reclassified into other areas, or because they become institutions of power working more and more within the established system (such is the tendency of labor unions) and henceforth furnish waiting places, locations that make possible another type of experience, or because their ideology no longer carries any weight since it fails to play an effective role in the life of the nation (in this way the policies of political parties evolve).[9]

Relating to this shift in the deep geography of the nation, "wildcat" protests offer a type of movement whose form is "cultural" because their participants can no longer make their requests clear within traditional sociopolitical frames of reference. A new set of social divisions, another conception of "politics," and new types of problems are put into play. Recently, we have seen American "instrumentalist" economy suspicious of theoretical models and trying out methods practiced in China through the adoption of the "direct method" (*tu-fa*), through a return to possibilities and to questions as they emerge from practice. In the same way, these "wildcat" protests can be taken as a point of departure, as the indication of ongoing changes, at the moment when global conceptions are no longer used.

Thus the action that aims at consolidating a "workers'" culture no longer corresponds to the desires expressed by the workers themselves, who wish to participate in the common culture, and who are scarcely disposed to letting themselves be enclosed in a single frame of reference.[10] Adhering to this archaic program means fixing in place the divisions created by a socioeconomic oppression in the nineteenth century; it means running against the grain of an evolution, and can also play into the hands of established ideologies or institutions.

We are witnessing the birth of associations that no longer follow the patterns of the same divisions. They reunite people who take public transportation or who use public parks to raise children, the inhabitants of a city polluted by nearby factories, vacationers exploited on beaches, and so on. They present a few characteristic features.

A new set of *social divisions* is emerging, corresponding to current relations between the power of decision and the law of consumption, rather than to the traditional lines of demarcation between workers and bourgeois, between manual workers and intellectual workers, and so on.

These groups are formed and identified by virtue of the newly discovered possibility of *being located somewhere,* in a relation to other forces. A conflict is made explicit within the system that formerly erased it. By dint of being distinguished from other positions, the members become capable of communicating with one another and of analyzing a concrete situation.

The turf on which new bonds are produced between the economic sphere (the situation of consumers) and the political sphere (the distribution of power) is defined *in cultural terms* (communication, leisure, habitat, etc.). New questions in a society thus find representation.

Here it is impossible to dissociate the act of understanding the environment and the desire to change it. "Culture" obtains one definition from it: we can state the meaning of a situation only as a function of *an action undertaken* in order to transform it. A social production is the condition of a cultural production.

With this particular case, there thus appears a type of cultural action that is pertinent in relation to global questions. Clearly, we are dealing with an unstable and often ephemeral phenomenon, for it cuts across existing institutions instead of gaining support from them. It is the symptom and the experimentation of a movement in the social geography, and not the prophecy of a solution or the example to be reproduced. But an independent language is torn off from the abstract universal of "culture." And why not, if not because it confronts powers and aims at transformation? It is based on both its own limits and those of other groups. It is embodied through its action.

Corresponding to this current type of cultural intervention are broader movements that cannot be circumscribed so easily. At least it is possible to designate the point from which they emerge. Incoherent as a group, they have the common trait of indicating a shift of acquired balances: formations of women, youth, or consumers, local groups (of regional, rural, or urban origin, etc.) present the qualities noted earlier. They do not fit into traditional categories. These units map out new, unofficial sites of cultural development.

One of the tasks of public service is to sustain their development. Capitalist methods of job enrichment—first used in certain American businesses and aimed at multiplying delegations of power and distributing responsibilities more broadly—can be tried. Better yet, self-constituting groups can themselves be furnished with the technical means that facilitate modes of social, and not merely cultural, experimentation.

2. Institutional Connections

Experience has shown that reforms introduced into institutions shaken by change (for example, the university) give way only to failures and aggravated difficulties. On the one hand, they assume that the institution provides a bedrock when in reality it has in part become the decor for other powers. The institutions indeed play on these fictions. On the other hand, they believe they are capable of injecting into certain areas, where degradation is most visible, different types of social therapy that are unlike what political action applies to the nation at large. But all the while the characteristic centralizing tendencies of contemporary societies "recuperate" these local oddities, forcing them back into the general system, but, along with the decay of these particular reforms, also bringing about the discredit of the very idea of a fundamental reform. Finally, they awaken resistances and inspire violent reactions because they call into question—with the visible part of an institutional unity—complex and deep-rooted phenomena that defy calculation. At stake, then, are measures out of which one or another policy can occasionally draw profit, but that in the long run are insufficient and often insurmountable.

In a general way, it has become impossible to contain the necessary changes within the framework of traditional organizations. That is how conclusions are reached at the expediency of ministries or organizations cut out according to the pattern offered by the evidence of increasingly important questions: culture, environment, and so on. This principle of *adjunction* has also ordered the creation of commissions or institutions at lower levels. Others are added, and institutional complements follow in their turn.

Here too experience is informative. These administrative outcroppings are dangerously linked to symptoms rather than to the reality of the problems they are supposed to remedy. Two types of difficulty are coming into view. On the one hand, the analysis of the initial cases reveals the breadth of the problems, their interference with areas that have long been reserved for other powers, the indefinite extension of allocated fields, and so on, in such a way that, in order to avoid disappearing into universalism, practical decisions are borne in the direction of immediate time and space. But the most accessible are often the most derisory. Activity is then divided into two equally disproportionate areas: considerations that are too broad and measures that are too narrow. On the other hand, former administrations, solidly in place and well positioned, resolve in their own areas problems that still depend on them and that, however, bear directly on culture or the environment: communications, city planning, teaching, television, and so on. What about subsidiary organizations? The fate of doing too little too late, and the role of bringing together the various types of nostalgia for a policy, the theatrical satisfactions given to the public, and the ineffective utopias developed through goodwill.

However, these measures do provide new openings and mark the need for official recognition, without which common interests would be eliminated, deprived of representations and powers. But at the institutional level, the most urgent action for adapting them consists in intervening in places where they find articulation. It is fixed upon the points where the very division into sectors can be reached, and thus the principles of their organization as well as their particular contents. This is *work on the borderlines.*

Actions will be all the more effective when they avoid further exemplarity, for the exception—even if it were contestatory—quickly, by way of being singled out, flows back into the commercial consumer system or into a system of political exploitation; it is caught in a crippling legendary list. On the contrary, the question entails creation at specific points of crisscrossings that allow institutions to account for the limits of their flexibility, their possible combinations, and, on the basis of *mixtures,* a few types of structuring that define a new society. The first goal is thus not of meeting "needs" (an illusory ambition itself based on the fiction of stable needs), but here too of using controlled intervention to build laboratories of social experimentation.

For the sake of identification, among these actions a few can be qualified that connect partitioned institutions (for example, permanent training), that are built on preexisting systems of relations (essentially, the city), that accelerate interference between social structures and cultural models (for example, in teaching, medicine, commercial enterprise, etc.).

The English "open university" is an example of the "institutional mix." Diffusion of production is assured through the linkages of television, printed materials, and private correspondence; it is combined with structures of reception that allow teachers or tutors to evaluate the activity inspired by distributed information, and "students" to establish locally personal relations with counselors. In the normal course of things, this totality brings into view some structural problems: thus the small proportion of workers enrolled as students is partially explained by the overly encyclopedic and abstract content of teaching, and the latter by constraints that are produced by the surrounding academic system. Or else, the exemplarity, the political role, and the celebrity of the experience promote a process of marginalization. Or, with a view toward avoiding it, a careful reaction is elicited on the part of directors. But the very interest of the operation consists in making clear the nature of the political decisions that have to be made, and in putting forward real possibilities.

A system of relations rather than a univocal place, *the city* requires a connection of spaces that are differentiated (because they are each defined by the societies that inhabit them) and yet hierarchized (to systems overlaid in the form of a "trellis" is added the sedimentation of historical systems). The abstract homogeneity of a single rationale is replaced by experiments that favor a structure of plurality in which, for example, the habitat of a minority is no longer understood as an abscess, but is recognized as one of many spatial modes of existence that cannot be isolated from others. If we assume that the city can be thought of and worked through not as a univocal language, but as a multiplicity of systems escaping the simple imperatives of a central authority, irreducible to a global formula, impossible to isolate from rural habitat, including economic organizations, but also systems that perceive the city as combinations of itineraries that make up urban practices, then a new type of society will be tested.

Finally, centers specializing in group dynamics, industrial psychology, or management will allow accelerated *interference between culture and labor.* For example, businesses can circulate cultural models by taking account of motivations, the use of the surrounding space, the development of collective participation, the diffusion of common values, and so on. In the same way, the analysis of changes at work in the socioprofessional figures of a society (those of the "militant," of the doctor who is a general practitioner, the military officer, the psychologist, etc.) brings them about. The blockages of certain organizations (especially universities) stem from resistances that are tied to earlier stages of institutional development, and that localize in discourse the values slowly driven out of social practice, such that, here—as in many liberal professions—ideological inflation at once betrays and arrests changes at work within the professional sector.

Politics and Culture

1. A Condition of Possibility: Political Power

We now have to get beyond both the technical questions envisaged up to now, and the operations that allowed their treatment, but we must not fall victim to the seductions of an ideology that now reappears in cultural garb. The broader problem of relations between cultural actions and political choices cannot be overlooked. Every single analysis, after having reviewed its data, weighs possibilities, proposes objectives, enters into the shadow cast by the powers that it calls into question; each analysis risks being arrested at that stage for lack of means in order to scale the cliff that it faces. Thus, each of these studies would eliminate the problem that they are all posing. Labor would become a plaything of society if it were always stopped at the moment it confronts the obstacle that seals off any passage in the direction of real social change. It would be equivalent to accepting the winnowing performed by the established powers in every project and that can only serve to assure their maintenance. Or else is it necessary to hold to revolutionary vows, to a literature as traditional as it is inoffensive?

It is clear that history is not made with conference papers. No matter what they say, they change nothing. At the very least, if they remain an instrument of social communication, they can make clear and put onto a common agenda the political responsibilities that citizens must assume at a time when too many cultural discourses would have us believe in the autonomy of "values" that the dominant powers are diffusing and reproducing with more means than ever at their disposal.

It is also clear that not everything has been said about culture when its current connection with the given order of trusts and castes is shown. Strictly speaking, nothing yet has been said about its nature. At least its function is elucidated and, furthermore, so is the condition of possibility for any change. From the Declaration of the Rights of Man to paid leaves, there has never been cultural innovation without social conflicts and political victories.

Certain people would go further. They think that cultural actions can be reduced to their implications and to their margin of sociopolitical profit, and, for example, that a festival is inconsequential if it is used by a reactionary government, or that a protest is futile if it is not part of a social struggle. That view is myopic. In a festival, as in an artistic creation, something exists that is not a means, but that is sufficient unto itself: the discovery of possibilities, the invention of encounters, the experience of these departures for "other places" — without which the atmosphere becomes stifling and seriousness amounts to everything that is boring about a society. How can a political "recuperation" ever grasp *that*, however successful or deft its means might be?

But, as long as a festival is subject to exclusions that excommunicate participants, or eliminate the presence of new forms, or withdraw connections that necessarily tie it to everyday life, the political question returns. It appears with these repressive limits that every social movement exceeds by constituting frames of reference. Politics does not assure happiness, nor does it give meaning to things. It creates or it refuses conditions of possibility. It prohibits or it allows; it makes possible or impossible. It is offered here from this point of view, insofar as cultural action collides with the interdictions that the powers set forth in silence.

2. The Relation with the Authorities

In a way equivalent to what folkore or popular culture had been, "mass culture" is forever marked by the social coeffecient that distinguished it from an operational culture that is always reserved. But we have noted that the break is aggravated. Mass culture no longer has a colonizing function (in both the good and bad senses of the word: at once civilizing and conquering), as was the case for more than two centuries for education, which diffused the conceptions of an elite by means of popularization. It became a malleable object that could reap profit according to the needs of production rather than as a military weapon.

Thus the relation with the authorities begins to change.[11] They exploit culture without compromise. They are elsewhere, far from involvement in the discourses they are fabricating. In France, powerful trusts diffuse all "cultural goods" that are sold or that assure the sale of other goods. They remain the owners of televised programs of their own manufacture that are diffused through the national television network. They control the press networks and even those of video. They finance centers of scientific research, both in and outside of the university, that work to meet their goals. They place their products according to requirements that are no longer those of the broad public simultaneously enabled to buy them and incapable of eluding their control.[12] In a word, the cultural commodities serve the class of those who create them and are bought by the mass of those who gain the least from them.

Conversely, by belonging to productive groups, people procure access to decision making. In order to obtain a position, a candidate gains little by studying computer programming unless it is in the service of a big corporation (IBM, etc.) or the army. Studying economics within the walls of the university does not lead far; by contrast, the red carpet rolls out through the elite schools surrounded by an almost familial network of "alums," members of upper financial, industrial, or political echelons. The same holds true at other levels. Social reasons dictate that competence or cultural training is no longer the road that leads to success—contrary to what an economic rationale would require—but the field that a group exploits or determines. Aspiring candidates have to work through the labyrinths of protectionism or monopolies. But surely it would be a mistake for them to take as a means of promotion the culture that these groups use as the theater of their expansion.

A cancer of the authorities, then, but "a healthy cancer." The authorities are organized independently of the body from which they draw their force and from which they gain no profit. They proliferate in the margins of the visible functionings of society. They secretly suck off the riches invested in the different sectors of culture — from national television to the countless institutions that recycle victims in the name of education or psychology.

3. A Necessary Politicization

With respect to these powers hidden in the social body, speech is more often than not a merely epidermal phenomenon. Just as in the political theater, statements rarely correspond to what is happening, and the spectrum of expression furnished on a daily basis to the public ostensibly shows that the energy of words spoken increases wherever their power diminishes. Moreover, however necessary it may be, the reintroduction of political problems in literary expression brings forth the sign of an urgency. But in itself, even if scandal or censure brings notoriety, that expression is sterile and without consequence.

Every one of the movements that have attempted to make a statement through collective "consciousness-raising" in similar situations — such as Paulo Freire's in Brazil — has run up against the same barrier. From the moment when, through its own process, an action begins to change the balance of forces, it is interrupted by repression organized by the established powers. Contrary to the "populist" hopes of strictly cultural organizations, the consciousness-raising retreats in view of inevitable political aggression. Beyond a threshold that is hidden or avoided, cultural promotion makes clear its necessary relation with the options that a society brings to bear upon itself, and with the unequal forces that each class uses to make its choices prevail.

In the so-called developed societies, conflicts do not arise unexpectedly. They are foreseen. Every cultural reaction that can give impetus to a shift of acquired positions seems to produce its countereffect. Thus the cultural centers that in principle can become sites of urban consciousness are displaced into theatrical productions and art centers, places where experts and directors (chosen by the guilds themselves) gather with a "cultivated" public. Youth centers, which once were conceived for political ends, become the means of enclosing a young population thought to be dangerous. In Belgium, technical schools and colleges that were created for workers are in fact especially used by instructors and the habitual clientele of university organizations so that the application procedures will replicate traditional structures...Countless examples can be cited. An entire system is revealed through them.

It goes back to the problem set forth at the beginning: as an expression, "cultural politics" camouflages the coherence that links a *depoliticized* culture with a *decultured* politics. The first is used for ends other than those it heralds. Politics as it is really practiced is subtracted from democratic, ideological, and cultural language; its official discourse reiterates banalities about national happiness and the new society, but its basic principles cannot be grasped, concealed as they are in the anonymous logic of a productivist and technocratic system.

This division between the explicit (a sterile language) and the implicit (powers that have become invisible) finally raises questions that are more political than cultural.

Will appropriations of operative culture be decided by rules established through the groups that own power? What structural change in society will allow a culture not to be divided into passive and active sectors according to social ranks, nor to shun professional training as one of its productive systems?

Will the groups that emerge from cultural passivity succeed in creating political forces? Will they succeed in modifying the geography of existing formations? Or, beyond a threshold of growth, will they perish because the present system could not care less about them? How to avoid letting the needed creativity of a society be slivered into "leisures" at a far remove from the powers that determine them, or in the form of marginalisms excluded from the active organization of the country?

In short, there can be no "cultural politics" unless sociocultural situations can be fashioned in terms of present forces and commonly known oppositions. It remains to be seen if the members of a society—today drowned in the anonymity of discourses of which they are dispossessed, and subject to conglomerates whose control exceeds their grasp—will find, along with the power of locating themselves in a game of acknowledged forces, the means of capturing speech.

Chapter 9
The Place from Which One Deals with Culture

Nothing *authorizes* me to speak of culture. I have no credentials for the task. Thus the positions I have taken figure, first of all, in different convictions and analyses. From that point, I can openly address a few of these threatening problems that "qualified" experts seek to avoid. An affected modesty would lead me directly into academicism.

Yet academicism has always been a fiction of universalism. A field of inquiry and its borders need to be staked out. I would like to devote a few sentences to a *site* of reflection on culture. Just as Arc-et-Senans is a place unlike many others, a specific place that would neither exclude nor consign to oblivion the multitude of those whom we cannot consider here, the work being done at Arc-et-Senans implies a situation that fate casts under the sign of particularity.[1] We thus cannot discuss culture or its global aspects without, first of all, recognizing the fact that we are are dealing with it from only one site, our own. It will be impossible either to eradicate or to overcome the alterity that experiences and observations, rooted in *other* places, hold before us and outside of us.

We therefore submit to the tacit law of a particular place. By *place* I mean the sum of determining factors that establish the limits of a meeting of specialists, a sum that circumscribes *with whom* and *about what* an exchange about matters of culture is possible. However scientific it may be, an analysis always amounts to a localized practice that produces only a regional discourse. It becomes serious insofar as it demarcates its limits by building its own field of inquiry on others that are irreducible.

From this site — the one from which we are dealing with culture — I shall only underline four determining features, which concern an objective, a technical specialization, a sociopolitical conditioning, and a European situation.

The Constraints of an Objective

This meeting has assigned itself less the task of redefining culture than of engaging "an action that needs to promote strategies of development." It is highly unlikely that any agreement will be reached about what actions ought to be undertaken. Contrary to analyses established in the homogeneous space of a technical field, action belongs to those who decide or to social forces that elude the grasp of observers. Furthermore, it cannot be dissociated from options and political ties that tend to determine observation. In other words, the agreement is not only improbable, but also doubly fictive. On the one hand, it would make an abstraction of *sociopolitical assumptions* on which are based a scientific appraisal and among which radical differences are clear. In one group exists a homogeneity that implies absences. The possibility of a discussion is based on excluded persons and forbidden topics; it is a fact, but a fact that needs to be known. It would be impossible to believe that these absences were insignificant. Discourse is even more determined through its axioms when it does not make them explicit. On the other hand, this agreement would assume that the discourses held by observers are the direct equivalent of the points of view of those who hold them, or are credited with a power of seduction, or miraculously supplement the forces that organize a nation. Discourse remains *foreign to action*, even when it talks about it.

If, then, a symposium is targeting an action, it cannot determine its objectives in any positive sense. But within this perspective, two tasks appear to be possible.

The first seeks to elucidate what cannot be eliminated from a serious study of this action, and what must not be granted privilege; that is, it seeks the clarification of conditions *without which* the spectrum of problems requiring solution would be shoddy, fallacious, or obsolete. In practice, that means opening up new hypotheses, breaking the barriers of interdiction, memory, or ignorance, and bending or overthrowing the objectives that appear to be, at a cursory glance, "obvious." The second aims at providing what are felt to be crucial issues with *concrete localizations*, mapping out relevant points of impact, projecting concrete hypotheses on the infrastructure of social life, and thus constituting a geography of possibility. The first task consists in doubting, in discerning, and in criticizing closures; the second, in creating and specifying openings. The agreement that is hoped for would thus locate the questions that need to be dealt with rather than furnishing answers to them.

There remains, even in the given format, a reflection or a writing on culture that suspends a decisive question: *who speaks, and to whom?* Every discourse is defined by a sender and a receiver. It assumes that both respect a tacit contract. More precisely, it is defined by determining the relations among interlocutors and auditors (or readers).

To whom, then, are the conclusions of this symposium addressed? To public opinion? To the ministers of cultural affairs?[2] To the various directors of cultural action? These multifarious receivers run the risk of vanishing into thin air, as do the discourses if they fail to reach their listeners. Words float, they are vacant, as long as they are not directed to specific ears. Such is the case for many texts and statements about culture in general. It seems to me that an analysis or a discourse fits into the "nowhere" of utopia if it does not define the field of its addressees and, in that very way, its own status.

The Limits of a Specialty: The Prospective

As specialists, none of us claims to speak in the name of "reality." The good days of that assurance are long gone. We now have to recognize in every scientific result the value of a *product*—such as what comes off the conveyor belt of a factory—relative to institutions, to axioms, and to procedures. Far from uttering truths, it is thus inscribed in one functioning among others. It refers to a specific place and to its own causes. It is inscribed in the logic of a *technical production*. There we find another form of limit. The prospective figures in the flags that fly over this symposium. It can furnish a few examples of borders and problems that inhere in the space of a discipline.

Current evolution of the prospective leads to a more narrowly circumscribed rationale and to recognizing to what degree the limited field of this rationale allows the infiltration of—and even appeals to—"a freedom of carnival," indeed, "crazy ideas" (Robert Jungk). Thus the Center for Behavior and Management Science at the University of Pennsylvania has abandoned projects that claimed to construct an architecture of stages to come and to eliminate its uncertainties from progress (cf. Russell L. Ackoff, *Corporate Planning*

[1971] or the works of Trist and Emery).[3] In their place is inserted a "style planning" that concerns "lifestyle" or the modes of behavior that can currently allow the expression of options acceptable for preservation. At the Tavistock Institute (London) that deals with operational research, a plan is hardly the description of future options that can be reached (surely that would be false); it is the way of expressing more correctly some choices and their criteria: it *stages* hypotheses indicated through analysis of the interconnections among fields of decision making (or "decision areas") defined by actors and their strategies.

These examples are only the symptoms of a tendency. Planning gets "theatricalized." It aims less at predicting the future (soothsayers and psychics are reserved for that) than in formulating *options* and conferring on them a possible *representation* in a socioeconomic language. It is in fact characteristic that, by criticizing its beginnings, the prospective rejects determining the future by this simple path that used to lead from analysis to decision along the line of a quantitative or technological continuum. A double revolution is at work here. The one changes the *method* and shatters the homogeneous discourse of observation through an *appeal to the imagination*. The other, more fundamental, modifies the *objective* and replaces the determination of a future with the *production of an operative discourse*. These two movements inject science with the need for fiction and for the priority of discourse. A sharpened consciousness of qualitative ruptures between the present and the future accords a growing importance to the imagination, and it removes from language the power of describing the future in order to endow it with the poetic function of stating options that today are rationally possible.

The future is no longer the object of scientific discourse; it is only marked by *current choices* for which discourse states the urgency or the opportunity. The future is an empty place that the prospective opens up on the basis of three current references: what is objectively *plausible*, what is subjectively *imaginable*, and what *can really be decided*. Essential to the prospective being mapped out are a practice of *difference* and a referral to *decisions* recognized as possible. Here we note two connected forms of an irreducible alterity: that of the future that remains unpredictable since it is different, and that of choices enacted today within a society. Through these characteristics, the new futurology cuts loose from the securities tied to the scientific positivism of the past. It recognizes its limits.

According to a broader determination, every analysis follows the codes of perception and "expectation" (Umberto Eco) that belong to a time and a place. We know that Christopher Columbus perceived the New World in the way the Canary Islands were described in chivalric novels. They classified the new in a given code. How could it be otherwise? In what way can we hope to change these implicit codes when, in every discipline, they represent the immanent law of the society in which a specialized discourse is written, and when, too, they constitute a sociocultural determination that serves as an axiom for every analysis that sets culture as its goal?

A Sociopolitical Condition

Rather than losing time over the determinations of a given specialty (the prospective), determinations that are essentially devoted to introducing the *qualitative* and *difference* into quantitative analyses and into the needed homogeneity of a calculus, I would prefer to underscore another, less explicit, limit: the sociocultural and political regionalism of our research on culture.

Despite theoretical and methodological divergences that can be brought to light in a meeting of professors and specialists, every group of investigators tends to reconstruct a unitary interpretation, to think of *culture in the singular*. It thus obeys the law of professional and social appurtenances. A homogeneity of milieu, class, and intellectuals is resurgent and betrayed by the very object (culture) in question. The place from which one speaks inside of a society silently reaches back into discourse and is itself represented at the level of intellectual content, with the reappearance of a *totalitarian* model. For *culture in the singular* expresses the *singularity of a place*. It is the way by which, in ideas, the authoritarian pressure of a social determination transpires, repeated and "reproduced" (Bourdieu and Passeron) even in scientific practice. In cultural analysis, the singular traces in bold letters the privilege of the norms and values that belong to a category.

For me this is a fundamental question. It summons the *place* that the intellectual occupies in society and a resulting experience or conception of culture. A case in point: what, on the one hand, is the relation between research that has enabled the members of liberal professions to gather at Arc-et-Senans and, on the other, the experience of an employee in a supermarket? What is offered to us as a salaried job consisting of pondering the conditions necessary for mastering change has an entirely different meaning for a workingwoman. What might be placed under the rubric of "culture" in her life would be *"doing something for oneself"* (and not for the boss), of *"going out"* (to the movies, on vacation, etc.), and of *"being with"* (family, relatives, etc.). Furthermore, as many recent studies have shown, she does not have the same relationship to language as do professionals of discourse; she does not *practice* language in the same way, for language is not the raw material of her labor, but rather, a point of reference for her activity. We would do well to wonder if the term "culture" is not purely equivocal. In any event, from where we are speaking, we are unable to overcome the difference that separates us from the experience of most people around us. We take the necessary risk of addressing the issue, but from the particular place that we inhabit and that determines our place in society.

Mention must also be made of the constraint imposed by the collective and personal origins of the very discipline that sets culture as its goal. An archaeology of institutions and "vocations" is still determining the fate of this activity: militant politics and pedagogical intentions discreetly inhabit researchers and turn them toward those who have the misfortune of being utterly different. An "evangelical" propaganda turns research into a concealed form of "white peace" (Robert Jaulin) — authoritarian conquest and pacification — in the name of particular criteria that groups that hold social power assume to be the condition of happiness and the definition of humankind. This philanthropy, alternately nostalgic and voracious, resembles a form of anthropophagia.

It would ultimately be illusory to assume that the most technical discussions are politically "neutral." Research is less and less free in relation to the state. Its financing, like the recruitment of research fellows, depends very directly on political objectives and concomitant social selections. On this score, the studies by the SIPRI (Stockholm, the works of Lettenberg, Clarke, etc.) are well known.[4] To be sure, on this topic self-censorship prevails. "We are in no way arguing for a political cause": such is the fairy tale that every scientific group rehearses by the evening fire. But an apologist would say that, in reality, "good" politics is being followed, a politics that needs neither to be explained nor chosen since it is already inscribed everywhere in the scientific institution. Or else, with a modesty that amounts to a kind of avowal, the slogan will be to "not be negative." Is this piece of courtesy possible when what is at issue is no longer the democratization of *one* culture, but rather of society at large?

I do not mean that somewhere we might find *a place* free of political shackles. That would be a pure fiction. My aim is different. It seeks to underscore the particularity of *our* place, and what dependencies, and hence choices or acceptances, are implied. *There is no observation that is not determined by the situation created by a relation*: the point has been established in different ways since Marx and Freud. Thus a group misconstrues the society in which it is inserted when it fails to recognize itself as a particular social category in the relations of production and in power relations.

European Closure

Generally speaking, in past societies that were culturally organized through frames of reference common to each group, but technically ill fit for communication among groups, the limit of every discourse was of the order of content; it held to an insufficiency of information, and not to an insecurity of local evidence. Things have since turned topsy-turvy. Information can be infinitely extended despite the effects of saturation being produced. In contrast, the choices and criteria appear to be local, not obvious, and uncertain. Common signifiers are referred to and used quite differently. *The limit strikes expression rather than content*. It marks the position of the group or of the subject, at the moment when it is erased from universally extended cultural signs. International information does not prevent a group from being *locally* determined. The universality of information is relativized through a peculiar way of being treated. This calls into question the *European* character of our discussion insofar as the topic of the debate implies a relation of Europe (but which one?) to other continents, or even a relation between European nations.

I shall assume only that the questions that the Third World puts before us are more fundamental. After others, perhaps more clearly than others, Georges Balandier has just shown that the processes of formation in "developing" countries question the systems of interpretation that industrial societies of both the East and the West ascribe to themselves. In this respect, the Third World does not merely furnish data supplementary to these interpretations, as if simply new variants were at stake. An epistemological suspicion is cast over our conceptions of the future of human societies, and thus over our own.

This observation does not involve systems of economic analysis (which are, by definition, closed) but their *functioning* in respect to systems of health or of schooling that do not fit their model. It thus relativizes historicosocial *global hypotheses* that are always put forward through the development or readjustments of our economies. Thus Western economic reason *works differently* in countries whose sociocultural structures are different from those that, over the past three centuries in Europe, have fostered the growth of technology and science. Surprising combinations among different systems are sketching out still unknown global hypotheses that might shift the general equilibrium of societies and ways of living or thinking that we have known.

This fact attests to the importance of historical and sociocultural substructures on which economic or cultural policies are based. Furthermore, it especially underscores a global fact that recoups the itinerary taken by innovators (Ivan Illich needed experience in Latin America to cast doubt on the excellence of the North American system).[5] The strangeness of our future does not have its essential source within, in the deployment of rational investigations or in the luxuriance of the imaginary. The future comes to us, sometimes unbeknownst to us, with formations, perhaps "anarchic and confused," of new and different worlds. Its principle resides in this confrontation.

Finally, the *other* society is the one in our time that opens up the rift of really different and future possibilities. No matter what, we are unable to "hold" its place. We have to situate ourselves in relation to other continents (and, as in Europe itself, in relation to social conflicts) in order to discern a future whose strangeness appears along with theirs.

What really characterizes Europe, with regard to other totalities, are the cultural heteronomies between each of the countries that compose it: a difference of languages, traditions, and histories still inhabited by a millennium of political and religious wars. To assign oneself a "European" definition of culture consists in using a purely oratorical gesture to neglect this omnipresent reality. It seems, to the contrary, that the elucidation of these divergences is the only possible way to discover a "European" specificity. For example, if we study closely the differences among these pasts, hidden systems that are unsuppressed by common urban or economic practices, a specifically

European type of combination might emerge, at the same time that the origin of more or less tacit resistances is met by univocal modes of reasoning. Thus it is worthwhile not to conceal the type of rationale that lives beneath the more "universal" propositions. Exhuming local propositions means creating for the most part a language of one's own, a langue that constitutes the reciprocal recognition of insurmountable alterities.

Through the clarification of what this colloquium seeks to identify with such precision, through the erosion of its "innocence," through the account it takes of its own assumptions, a relation of veracity can be established between the form of discussion and the content of the object that is being discussed. Indeed, it seems to me—and this was the topic of these scattered reflections on the "site" of Arc-et-Senans—that nothing serious can be proposed without simultaneously making clear the peculiarity of this meeting and the need to relate it to sites, to forces, and to analyses other than our own. *In short, the future enters the present in the mode of alterities.* The confrontation with others is the principle governing any prospective. That means finding, moreover, the law that, with the coming of sexuality, makes the genesis of life depend on a relation with others.

Chapter 10
Conclusion
Spaces and Practices

The Soft and the Hard

A first impression, a persisting malaise: culture is *soft*. Analysis slips everywhere over the uncertainty that proliferates in the gaps of prediction as soon as the certainty of the illusory statistics of objective signs (behavior, images, etc.) slips away. Thus the *styles or ways of practicing space* flee the control of city planners. Able and ready to create a composition of places, of full and empty areas that allow or forbid passage, city planners are incapable of imposing the rationality of reinforced concrete on multiple and fluid cultural systems that organize the living space of inner areas (apartments, stairways, and the like) or public domains (streets, squares, etc.) and that innervate them with an infinite number of itineraries.[1] They concoct and map out an empty city, leaving it when the inhabitants come, as if they are savages who will, without their consent, turn topsy-turvy the designs they had made.

The same holds true for ways of living time, reading texts, or seeing images. What a practice does with prefabricated signs, what the latter become for those who use or receive them — there is an essential point that still remains, for the most part, unknown. It produces movements or stagnations that a mere analysis of signifiers can never grasp: collapses, displacements, or a hardening mentality; continuing patterns of traditional behavior beneath their outer metamorphosis, or mutations of their meaning despite an appearance of objective stability; distortions of "values" invested in the life of a group without its needing to make them explicit, and so on. What can be measured everywhere meets this mobile element along its borders. Calculation comes into play (fixing a cost for the death of a human being, a tradi-

133

tion, or a landscape), but gets drowned. The management of a society leaves in its midst an enormous "remainder." On our maps, *that* is what is called culture. It is an ebb and flow of muffled voices on the architects' blueprints in their advanced stages of drafting.

In fact, this soft region is silently exploited by its opposite, the *hard*. Culture is the battlefield of a new colonialism; it is the colonized of the twentieth century. Contemporary technocracies install whole empires on it, in the same way that European nations occupied disarmed continents in the nineteenth century. Corporate trusts rationalize and turn the manufacture of signifiers into a profitable enterprise. They fill the immense, disarmed, and almost somnolent space of culture with their commodities. All forms of need, all the rifts of desire get "covered," that is, inventoried, dealt with, and exploited by the media. This economic system erodes and ultimately inverts the political experience acquired in the nineteenth century, replacing the act of democratic representation with the reception of standardized signifiers that destine workers to become consumers, and that turn people into a public mass.

Economic imperialism, a violent *conquista* of the cultural market, has a comic doublet: politics, which has become for us a decorum of former ideologies behind which are advancing new technocratic and managerial powers.[2] Behind this facade the colonialism of the trusts is rehearsed but in a derisory way. When the "political authorities" do not acknowledge the powers they serve, or when they try to conceal the idiocy of their own programs (which can be summed up in the slogan "Get rich! Get rich!"), they deploy the rhetoric of "values" exhumed from the past; they display loquacious "humanisms" where tales of the fears of the well-off are told. They establish fragile militias of "animators" devoted to camouflaging the contradictions of a regime.

From then on, culture appears as the field of a multiform battle between the forces of the soft and the hard. It is the outrageous, cancerous symptom of a society divided between the technocratization of economic progress and the folklorization of civic expression. It makes manifest an inner dysfunction: the fact that the appropriation of productive power by privileged organisms has as a corollary a political disappropriation and regression of the country, that is, the disappearance of the democratic power to determine the organization and representation of the labors that a society exerts on itself.

A Pathological Zone

The abandoned lot of culture is the place where tensions and social ills make themselves known. In place of immediate interventions ordered by interest groups, instead of the solemn stupidities that are invoked today in the name of "man" or of "values," a therapeutics first of all calls for some observations in the form of *clinical pictures.*

I have presented here only a few cases limited to France. It is nothing, if we think of the hexagon as a little world locked in on itself. But, in its cultural sector, we already can see the pathological symptoms piling up, like pimples and rashes on the body. Thus the challenges and the sundering revisions tied to the logic of development favor at once the ambition of young wolves, students of business administration, and managers of reformism; Poujadism[3] and corporatisms fostered by fears of insecurity; the stiffening of ideologies born in former times, or the regression of conservatives to religious languages in which they no longer believe. The boredom of adults in professional sectors is rehearsed in the boredom in schools, and it extends into the passivity experienced in leisure activities. These are the signs of a sickness that appears depressive.

The vivid colors are fading. This country has acquired a stone gray color. Dull tones prevail. What can be offered to remedy the situation? What can all the chatter, following the battles of other times, buzzing in the newspapers day after day, ever do to help? Or the stupid niceties of the "good, good" little world that the Club Meds offer to their clientele of singles and burnouts? In the streets are amassed men who fret over having lost a sense of festival and play. Two major concerns seem to motivate their lives: *get rich* and *firm up.* Tropisms of soft bellies.

At the same time that the taste for risk is lost, so also are the very reasons for living. And nothing controls from within the sweet and monstrous expansion of wealth. The sheltering of profit and knowledge, hexagonal chauvinism at its best, the repression of foreigners and things foreign, are endlessly engendered in a directly inverse relation. Behind the proprietary instinct appears the most ignominious of all human faces: racism.

What could be more astonishing if, in the upper echelons, the cult of the past were defining programs of cultural education, and if political conformism became the criterion of creativity? The order that fills our streets with police would also seek to have statues of the dead perched at every corner in our parks and gardens, and have calmly edifying works shown in our theaters, museums, and bookstores.

The French Theater

The corrective of a massive phenomenon has to be added to this dim picture. The spectacles that the mass media fabricate are no longer representing the French. They are no longer organizing a space where convictions get expressed, circulated, or confront each other. *Exit populus.* The population withdraws. It loses all sense of function.

Some extreme signs are beginning to multiply: "refusal to consume," exile to foreign countries, retreat into the hinterlands, formation of splinter groups, communes, or assemblies that are sick of grazing on the pastures of ideology, and so on.

In a more general sense, the press, radio, and television are turning into *theaters*, just like what in everyday life is called the "political theater." The spectator with a thousand eyes appreciates the style and the performance of the actors but no longer believes in the stories they are telling. "Geraldine Chaplin was simply great!" "Pompidou was a nerd!" Behind the character, the gaze discovers the actor. In the distance taken from the image, the public perceives the conditions of its production. It evaluates the way it is made without going after its content. The text becomes the material exploited by an art of staging. Thus pictures and discourses appear as if they were something slick — in the talents, techniques, or rules that give birth to them and are clearly shown — much more than convictions or truths. What comes out of all the mass media, both for the public and for the producers, is a generalization of the *rhetoric,* even if it can be said that the latter essentially consists in taking discourses (verbal, iconic, or gestural) to be a function of the "ways of doing" that produce their effects.

It can no longer be presumed that these discourses are "expressive" of those who read, see, or hear them. The analyses by the press or television reporter that summon public opinion wrongly skip over the distance that the latter establishes between itself and its pleasures.[4] The public *is no longer there*; it is no longer circulating in these images or caught in their traps; it is elsewhere, in the background, assuming the position of an amused, interested, or bored receiver. Thus it has fewer and fewer places of its own, insofar as the entire language becomes more and more theatrical. For the purpose of obtaining an inkling of what the receivers of serialized messages may be, what they think, or what they desire, polls begin to multiply. Market research of this kind only yields answers by respondents who "play" with the questions; from the polls are extracted only the fragments of the theatricalization in which it is playing a role; the polls no longer affect the people who slip away and disappear into unknown realms behind the "reactions" of a "public" that is now and again called upon to walk onto the stage of a national commedia dell'arte.[5]

Probably this is the most important and paradoxical consequence of the development of the mass media. A rift is produced between what is said (but is not real) and what is experienced (but cannot be put into words). Language becomes a fiction in relation to an everyday reality that has no language. In the society of spectacle, the surfeit of signifiers betrays an impossibility of finding any adequate expression. Messages abound, saturating the atmosphere, and every day the dumpsters of every city have to be emptied; but the drone and buzz of information create an absence of speech.

Is it by chance that psychoanalysis is turning into a cultural esperanto, furnishing the West with a vocabulary, in itself metaphorical, of what our own language is *becoming*? It sends representations back to their conditions of production, and refers statements to an unstated condition. Escaping the control of specialists, and constituting a new myth[6]—but disseminated into a vocabulary—the Freudian lexicon socially designates the state in which language functions; it connotes the relation of discourses with a repressed dimension of communication. It is indicative of the system in which the more language proliferates, the less we say.

Permanences: The Borderline of a Silence

Seen in these interconnected aspects, culture oscillates more fundamentally between two forms, in which the one endlessly casts the other into oblivion. On the one side is what "permanates"; on the other, what is invented. On the one hand, there are slowly developing phenomena, latencies, delays that are piled up in the thick breadth of mentalities, evident things and social ritualizations, an opaque, stubborn life buried in everyday gestures that are at the same time both immediate and millenary. On the other hand, irruptions, deviations, that is, all these margins of an inventiveness from which future generations will sucessively draw their "cultivated culture." Culture is an untold night in which the revolutions of earlier times are dormant, invisible, folded into practices—but fireflies, and sometimes great nocturnal birds, cutting through it—as thrusts and creations that trace the promise of another day to come.

This oceanic night fascinates me but also interrogates me. It is the humanity that everyone lives unbeknownst to oneself. The sleep in which we speak unaware of ourselves. History and sociology, economics and politics only catch hold of the "resistances." Because scientific or governmental action is always elitist, it falls upon the silent culture of collectivity as an obstacle, a neutralization, or a dysfunction of its own projects. What is perceptible in it is thus an "inertia" on the part of the masses with respect to the crusade of an elite. It is a *limit*. The "progress" of clerks or directors stops at the shores of a sea. This mobile borderline separates men who are in power from "the others."

But this vision is the *effect* of a class relation. It assumes as "other," as an unknown, menacing, or seductive horizon, everything that fails to conform to the practices and ideas of a milieu. "Passivity" and "resistance" are concepts that are *relative* to the place where "progress" is accredited with representation, where the means of deploying a conquering interventionism are exercised. Can this situation be modified in our time? Under what conditions can the relationship of forces that constitutes the majority at the limit of its action over the minority be changed?

Technical procedures have been used to address this question. Thus voices that had never been heard have been recorded and lost in the molten type of print shops: the voices of the Sanchez children in Mexico, the voice of the old fugitive slave, Esteban, the voice of the peasant revolutionaries of a Chinese village . . .[7]

Experiences, ambitions, and anger unknown to us speak in the first person. They are no longer the object constituted by an ethnologist's gaze. In *Let Us Now Praise Famous Men*, James Agee wanted to go even further.[8] Instead of collecting the words of the others, he wanted to put together pieces of wood, slivers of broken pottery, leftovers, in a word, the dispersed fragments of other languages. A marvelous and impossible project, this collage, organized around something that was missing, would have created an absence, but without filling its space with the products of our knowledge. Unfortunately, this is only a utopia, since these windows opened onto the other only function like a diorama in trompe l'oeil perspective. They are absorbed and turned into folklore by the context in which they are inscribed. It is scarcely the sign of an investigation, a mark left by the other.

Thus this limit ought to be accepted as a question *and* its answer. Analyses pertaining to culture move along the edge of a silent immensity. In walking over the beaches of the inaccessible, they discover their irreducible limits and, in that way, their relation to a dead form. Obsessed by this murmur of the other country, I must recognize that no text or institution could ever "hold" to the place where the drone of machines continues to murmur, where the noise of tools, kitchens, and a thousand and one creative activities is heard. These infinite lexicons and foreign vocabularies are silenced as soon as the museum or writing seizes these fragments in order to make them speak in our interests. At that point they cease to speak and to be spoken. All the progress of our knowledge can be measured by the silence that it creates. What therefore is the borderline that allows the passage into our culture of only the fallen, extracted, or inert signs of another culture?

This borderline circumscribes what we can say and make of the place from which we are speaking. Nothing from other cultures crosses this barrier without coming to us dead on arrival. Whatever exists is what irreducibly escapes us. The theory and practice of culture accede to honesty when we cast away the pretension of overcoming, by way of generalities, the rift that separates the places where an experience or an event can be uttered. From scientific knowledge (when it is exclusive), all the way up to indigent discourses on "values" or on "humanism," countless ways of eliminating other existences can be named. The common trait is that of the drive to establish unity, that is, a totalizing vision. Culture in the singular always imposes the law of a power. A resistance needs to be directed against the expansion of a force that unifies by colonizing, and that denies at once its own limits and those of others. At stake is a necessary relation of every cultural production with death that limits it and with the battle that defends it. Culture in the plural endlessly calls for a need to struggle.

A Creative Swarm

Every culture proliferates along its margins. Irruptions take place that are called "creations" in relation to stagnancies. Bubbling out of swamps and bogs, a thousand flashes at once scintillate and are extinguished all over the surface of a society. In the official imaginary, they are noted only as exceptions or marginal events. An ideology of property isolates the "author," the "creator," and the "work." In reality, creation is a disseminated proliferation. It swarms and throbs. A polymorphous carnival infiltrates everywhere, a celebration both in the streets and in the homes for those who are unblinded by the aristocratic and museological model of *durable* production.[9] The origin for this model is a mourning and its effect is a lure. The apologia of the "imperishable" valorizes the dead rather than the living, resistant materials rather than others, and impoverished places for the sake of ensuring the consecration of their relics. But the inverse is the case. Creation is perishable; it passes because it is an act.

On the other hand, it cannot exist without a relation to a collectivity. That alone can allow it to become durable. The "humanist" conception encloses it in a vicious circle that indefinitely refers to the perishable individuality of the author and the permanence of the completed and self-contained work. It believes in a resurrection based on private property. In fact, what is creative is the gesture that allows a group to invent itself. It mediates a collective operation. Its trace will possibly outlive the group by assuming the form of an object fallen from life, taken, left aside once more, and then redeployed for later practices: texts, pottery, tools, or statues. But this no longer belongs to what is *making* history; rather, it is one of its *givens*.

Furthermore, today we distinguish *what* is written (what is *spoken*) from the *gesture* that produces it (the act of *speaking*).[10] This tendency no doubt plays a role in our cultural experience, which refers systems of signifiers to procedures or to the act of which they are a result—a statement having expression. In any event, this return to production gives to expression its function of working for the formation or renewal of a group. The goal of a rock concert, a play, a public gathering, and so on, is less one of peeling the immemorial truth from its laminations in a work than of allowing a collectivity to be constituted through the act of self-representation. Its collective gesture is something *marginal* in relation to former practices. It is also a productive *act* and, if it stages various and diverse functions, it no longer obeys a law that separates actors from spectators. This, at least, is the direction that current research is taking. In this coproduction, expression in language is a movement that accompanies and locates a passage of the collectivity. It is integrated in the common gestures of "taking off," of leaving, and of "traveling" (taking a trip). It is the common ground of a collective "ecstasy," of an "exile" assembled together, of a celebration. From the "evening out" organized by friends, a family, or a group of youths, to the theatrical, popular, or revolutionary "demonstration," a common element, essential to these expressions, prevails: *a social group is produced by producing a language.* The celebration cannot be reduced to the recordings or to the remainders it leaves behind. However interesting they may be, these "cultural" objects merely amount to the residue of what no longer exists, namely, the expression or the work—in the full sense of the term.

Thus linked to the social operation it is building, the work perishes with the present it symbolizes. It is not defined by its need to survive, as if the goal of the labors of a collectivity on itself were to fill museums. To the contrary, the work is the metaphor of a communicative act destined to blow to smithereens and thus allow other expressions of the same kind, further removed in time, on the basis of other momentary contracts. Far from being identified with what is rare, solid, costly, or "definitive" (the traits of a masterpiece, which is a patent), it aims to vanish in what it materializes.

From this result two important aspects of culture. On the one hand, caught in the ephemeral collective link whose moment of possibility it crystallizes—and destined to disappear with it—cultural expression concerns both the *instant* that it marks and a *death* to which it returns. It represents a risk that cannot be arrested in the flight of its signs, as might a bird metamorphosed in stone.

In other words, a work cannot be grasped when the laws that unconsciously control it are exhumed. At stake are merely the structures from which it emerges by continuing to signify them. But it exists precisely along the interstice or the margin that it opens up, all the while continuing to live under the order of social, psychological, and linguistic laws. It insinuates a surplus, an excess, and thus also a rift in the systems that at once lend support to it and to its conditions of possibility. A day is built in a constructed space. The latter displaces the equilibrium of the former without, however, escaping it. A space of play is introduced. There are the streaks of a buffoonery: an amusement, a transgression, a "metaphorical" voyage, a passage from one order to another, a fugacious oblivion within the great orthodoxies of memory. All these movements are related to organizations and to continuities. But they also fold into it the modest proliferation of a creativity. The ways that creativity gnaws at the margins of legal texts speaks to the most fragile and essential components of *human* activity. The infinite *variant* that grows massively, like a fungus, in the cracks between the micro- and macrophysical orders—such is our *culture*.

On the other hand, a "literary" or "artistic" (in other words, elite) form could never establish the norms of culture that this practice of marginality assumes. In this way, a particular milieu imposes on everyone the name of *the* law, which in reality is only *its* law. A privileged class thus invests its power in education and culture. It abusively valorizes the instruments and raw materials of uses, in the same way that it deploys its possibility of disposing of time. A typewriter, some paper, and a little leisure: this little world would, for example, circumscribe the site in which art can be born. But housing, clothing, housework, cooking, and an infinite number of rural, urban, family, or amical activities, the multiple forms of professional work, are also the ground on which creation everywhere blossoms. Daily life is scattered with marvels, a froth on the long rhythms of language and history that is as dazzling as that of writers and artists. Lacking proper names, all kinds of language give birth to these ephemeral celebrations that surge up, disappear, and return.

Yet one has to wonder why these cultural expressions produced with the vocabulary of tools, utensils, clothing, or everyday gestures seem to be silenced at the doorways to factories and offices. In places where production is concentrated, creativity seems merely to be shameful, camouflaged in the minimal technical improvements that the professional competence of workers can inject into the norms the management imposes. In these areas, it is limited to the managerial staff, the engineers, and the directors. It is forbidden to others. The possibility for creation begins only at a certain social level, and is not allowed for the "lower" orders, specifically to those who produce. The business or the administration speaks the truth about a system when it makes brutally clear the division between "producers" and "creators." It sets forth the principle reproduced by the bourgeois ideologies that organize educational or cultural policies. The appropriation of creation on the part of the privileged elite, the gods in the pantheon of capitalism, reverberates throughout the entire society, beginning with the economic citadel of their power, that is, with the centers of production. In the consumer sectors (leisure, habitat, home repairs, etc.), this power can allow creativity to flow without being threatened. On the contrary, it draws profit from them.

With the strike at the Fiat factory in 1970, or with the collective management of the Lip watch factory in 1973, we have an indication of the real stakes of culture and of the struggle necessary for its transformation.[11] The workers at Fiat claimed the right to use their trademark, to introduce their ideas and their "poetic" variants into the manufacture of cars—in a word, *the right to be creators.* This amounted to fundamentally challenging the capitalist abstraction of which only one reflection is found in the ideology that limits creators to an intelligentsia of artists or writers. Based on a problem in employment, the workers at Lip demanded the right to participate in the socioeconomic management of their enterprise. Some aimed directly at changing the goods; others, at the form of their production. They assumed the responsibility for the same problem from both ends, input and output, even if it is true that a production of signs is the mode by which a collective group produces its identity.

Some Cultural Operations

In every instance, techniques of expression (whether theatrical or done by hand, whether literary or professional) are integrated into a social practice. The use of a tape recorder, the organicity needed for the team that is making a documentary, the agreements articulated on cable television turn expression into the means by which a group is defined, acquires its sense of identity, and becomes the subject of its own history. Here innovation is not limited to the modernity of the media being used, even if the latter multiply the possibilities of creation; it resides in the uses to which they are put. Yet, however important they may be by their own nature, these experiments remain adjacent and symbolic as long as they are unable to find their effectiveness in the areas of productive labor and socioeconomic organization.

No matter what these modalities are, cultural *expression* is, above all, an operation. Furthermore, the thematic strands of current research offer an initial description. Three points are especially striking: (1) *to do something with something;* (2) *to do something with someone;* (3) *to change everyday reality* and modify one's lifestyle to the point of risking existence itself. In that way, turning away from a network of issues concerned with representations and toward the exceptional character of the expression being "cultivated," we move toward a perspective centered on practices, on human relations, and on the transformation of the structures of social life. The *operative, illocutionary*, the *"trivial"* (which is also fundamental): such is the hub of the cultural revolution sketched out at the base and disseminated in the innovations that swarm at grassroots levels.

Through this work, theoretical tasks are brought into view. Thus, it would be useless to seek a solution to the incertitude of the relation that cultural "creation" holds with its "reception." The very terms of the question need to be revised. Reserving the creative act to the particular form that it takes among the elite of a society is the social a priori of this way of posing the problem. The ruse of the question consists in eliminating beforehand, along with the idea of "reception," the hypothesis of creativity other than that of the producers who are in power or who occupy a favored milieu.

No less admissible are the presuppositions of an analysis that is arrested on the product, for example, on the text, and that neglects the praxis of reading. It is blind, "forgetting" at least two essential problems. On the one hand, meaning of a text is the effect of intepretative procedures applied to the surface of the text. Thus, the permanence of texts becomes a secondary element next to disparate ways of reading them, since the latter themselves also affect the same cultural objects with heterogeneous meanings. The cultural value of the same piece of writing or the same street varies according to the use that is made of it, that is, according to textual or urban practices.[12] On the other hand, the ideology that claims to stick to the text and let it speak is unaware of its own functioning. It camouflages the exclusivity that it assures to reading practices confined to a given milieu. What it *states* conceals what it *does*, namely, prohibit all other interpretative practices.

Reading is only one case among others, but it indicates that a more general rift divides a study fixed on the products and an analysis of operations. There, already, in the field circumscribed by the experience of reading, as soon as a textual practice (whether of the televised image, of the street, etc.) encounters research, real problems arise. Thus, the homogenization of cultural products due to the rationalization of their production no longer obliterates the more important compensatory phenomenon of a masked differentiation of interpretative actions. With the progressive unification of objects, the heterogeneity of practices can be taken seriously and, along with it, the effectiveness of a culture that has shattered into pieces.

Another question arises: we have to quit thinking that a qualitative gap exists between the acts of reading and writing. The first is a silent creativity invested in what the reader does with the text; the second is this very creativity, but made explicit in the production of a new text. Already present in reading, cultural activity merely finds a variant and a prolongation in writing. From the one to the other, no line of difference separates passivity from activity, except the line that distinguishes different ways or styles of socially *marking* the gap opened up by a practice in a given form. What is needed in order for this mark to be literary, in order to make the interpretative operation explicit in cultivated language, are a particular training, leisure time, a place in the intelligentsia, and so on. The difference is *sociological*. Rather than giving way to the psittacism of a division between active and passive elements, it is worth analyzing how the cultural operation is modulated on different registers of the social pattern at large, and what are the methods by which this operation can be favored.

Generally speaking, the cultural operation might be represented as a *trajectory* relating to the *places* that determine its conditions of possibility. It is the *practice of a space* that is already constructed when it introduces an innovation or a displacement. By "places" I mean the determined and differentiated places organized by the economic system, social hierarchies, the various types of syntax in a language, traditions of custom and mentality, psychological structures. For three-quarters of a century, the development of the human sciences can almost be identified with the exhuming of the coherences and contracts that form the architecture of social life, whether individual or collective. Moreover, science only followed and made manifest the movement of our Western societies. But, in making vast diagrams of these synchronisms, it neglected the operations that cut through them. Despite Marxist tradition, praxis was removed from the *object* under study, probably because it was internal and reserved for the productive *subject* of science, that is, the specialized groups and milieus to which they belonged. In any event, today we have a surfeit of knowledge and methods as far as structures are concerned, and we are impoverished as soon as we have to study operations, transformations, in short, movement.

Thus, cultural operations are movements. They inscribe *creations in coherences* that are both legal and contractual. They stipple and trace them with trajectories that are not indeterminate but that are unsuspected, that deform, erode, and slowly change the equilibrium of social constellations.

It appears to me that in cultural matters we have to direct our research toward these operations. That means, while using them, that we go beyond the works that oscillate between consideration of the *message* (content: themes, mental objects, values, etc.) and the refinement of the *media* (forms and modes of communication). Among the tasks that can correspond to this orientation, I will indicate only two that might have as their goals to grasp the relation of operations and systems, and to map meaningful formations on their production.

First of all, the very possibility of these operations implies that the systems are no longer understood as stable objects under the unrelenting gaze of a discipline. This discipline is based on a position of force. It takes for granted that a bourgeois class or a European society owns the perpetual concession of the privileged position that it occupies. Systems appear more as structures being moved about than equilibriums of forces in conflict.

Science itself is hardly autonomous with respect to these conflicts and participates in their reincarnations. If it is thus — but that requires taking up over and again the dialectics elaborated by and since Marx — then a grid of these forces gives way to operations that no longer need to be pigeonholed in the utopian no-man's-land of ungrounded spontaneity.

Above all (and this is a corollary, but an important one), the phenomenological and praxiological analysis of cultural trajectories must allow to be grasped at once a composition of places and the innovation that modifies it by dint of moving and cutting across them. The evolution of a pedagogical experiment, of a gathering place for youth, of a theatrical troupe, or of a self-managed community encounters resistance of different kinds, but it brings into view the qualitative thresholds in its duration or in its spatial extension, and so forth. It reveals "places" by dint of capturing them. Only an action is able to bring forth what had been hidden in the opacity of social life. An intervention is already "cultural" in the way it emerges from the shadows, producing effects of social representation and transformation. Yet, by virtue of this discovery, other future effects can better be calculated; operative rules can be determined; use can be made of the game allowed by the articulation of different social and mental places; the events that make possible a bilocation (that is, a double belonging that makes one place "work" on another) can be predicted; but, too, the limits can be recognized beyond which this game becomes either a perversion that no longer touches on real things or a transgression that provokes a rejection.

In this way, a cultural tactic becomes possible. It apportions to quantifiable givens an unquantifiable risk—that of existing, which no ideology of "values" or of "Man" could ever be able to cover. The analysis and practice of innovation in our constructed spaces do not touch on the essential point, which is also the most fragile: a desire to live while losing the assurances that every society multiplies— a madness of being. Culture is only analogous to the wisdom that Don Juan, Castañeda's Yaqui sorcerer, defined—in the sense that we "inspect" a car—as the art of *inspecting one's madness*.[13]

Afterword
A Creative Swarm
Tom Conley

La culture au pluriel is a founding charter for culture studies. Its ten essays map out a field that has exploded into life in the two decades following their writing.[1] It is both inspiring and depressing to discover that what Luce Giard has carefully revised and emended for this edition first appeared in the midst of the revolts of 1968 and their aftermath. Inspiring, because the book constitutes a living testimony to the origin and the implementation of "ways of doing things," to practices, to creative styles of thinking and working in the unkind and degraded world in which we are born, live, and cope. The essays tell us how to sift through many of the specious truths we have inherited in the name of culture. Depressing, because the diagnostic that the author advances, if it has been heard outside of France, has been confined to areas — mostly in programs of literary and comparative theory — where actions and policies recommended to change the world are stagnantly virtual. If action is initiated, it is restricted to the space of classrooms and coffee tables. Even if the writings have inspired different ways of thinking, the pluralization that Michel de Certeau sought to implement in the years 1968–73 remains to be legislated.

Two bright signs accompany the English translation of *Culture in the Plural* and its companion volume, *The Capture of Speech and Other Political Writings*. The works may be the first of their kind to bridge theoretical and practical spheres of activity. Whereas *The Capture of Speech* asks how people can obtain agency when they have no power of speech to think or act on their destinies, *Culture in the Plural* goes a step further by advocating pedagogies and practices that pluralize communication. Both volumes appeal as much to theorists of space and to geographers as to applied sociologists, to cadets of Lacanian

149

psychoanalysis, and to historians of religion. The books engage ways of changing the world, but also, in the traces of the itinerary the author draws through a welter of local dilemmas, they betray how dialogue about society and environments can begin in different contexts and places.

Some of the conflicts that inspire the writings have been dulled or forgotten. The stakes of speech in 1968; the socialization of the Lip watch factory; minority identities and the secessionist movement for a free Brittany; Herbert Marcuse's utopia of social reorganization in the midst of opulent wealth around the military complex of San Diego; the plight of the French university during postwar demographic expansion; the opposition of elite and mass culture imposed on the French secondary schools. But no matter. Whatever the issue may be, Certeau begins from a given context before addressing cultures at large. Some of the resonant themes include how to develop dissonant voices within the language of dominant culture; ways of welcoming the immigrant or the other in one's own society; the relation of habitus and conflict in social space; how to make secondary and advanced education available to everyone, but so that popular cultures obtain legitimate places in the architectures of knowledge; means of producing "creative swarms" in the four cultural worlds in which we live.[2]

The other bright sign is found at the end of *Culture in the Plural*, where Certeau gives us a rudimentary and compelling plan that can inspire collective programs of cultural studies: any expression that bears on life at large, he concludes, builds from a need "(1) to do something with something; (2) to do something with someone; (3) to change everyday reality and modify one's lifestyle to the point of risking existence itself." As in any paradigm of lasting design, axiomatic questions of this type forever need to be kept in view. Spelled out as they are, they constitute a point of departure and return for all the given issues.

Trained as a historian of religion, the author of *Culture in the Plural* applies principles of cultural transmission to empirical disciplines. In his work on early modern religion, Certeau studied the relation of belief to social action. Yet because, for the greater part of his life, he wore no institutional badge, Michel de Certeau's views on culture do not resemble the wealth of writings that have multiplied over the last decade on the decolonizations of race, class, and gender. One of his commanding hypotheses is that "culture" needs to be understood not as a monument celebrating human mastery of nature but, to the contrary, and more modestly, as collective ways or *manners* of thinking and doing. Diversity of origin stands at the basis of any definition of culture. It is marked by heterogeneity of practices, styles, modes, or fashions of selectively and affectively producing (but not arrogating) habitable space. Understood thus, cultures are inflected as collective and anonymous ways of meshing social and natural environments in the process of living. Cultures are always pliable, changing shape to avoid containment by structures imposed from without. They are processes shared by *people,* and they work surreptitiously in the midst of codes that define a *public.*

For Certeau, a principal task of cultural studies entails elaborating codes that develop specific ways of inventing life as it is lived from year and month to day and hour and minute. His initial work in this area is best known in North America through *The Practice of Everyday Life* (English edition, 1984), a book that shares with *Culture in the Plural* the idea that "spatial practices" can mobilize cultures in the direction of those who have no means to obtain even the most remote feelings of community. Some of the most dazzling pages of *The Practice of Everyday Life* show how people, driven by an innate sense of poetry, choose to map out their daily promenades.[3] Certain individuals the author knew in Paris encrusted their itineraries with shards of preconscious languages elicited by concurrent impressions of the jagged and accidental aspect of the streets. Thus Certeau called the spatial practice of walking "the awakening of inert objects . . . that, bereft of their stability, change the place in which they were inhumed into the uncanniness of a space of their own."[4] Certeau's words sum up what he said about a friend—was he the author or the creation of an intimate other?—who lived in Sèvres, comes to Paris, wanders about the sixth arrondissement, and moves "toward the streets of *Saints-Pères* and *Sèvres,*" while en route to see his mother in another quarter. His feet allow him to articulate a statement with these names, but the event takes place completely unbeknownst to him. Something *other* is happening in this parable of language mobilized on the sidewalks, not only for the man from Sèvres, but also for us, in the space opened up between its narration and its reception.

But what is it? *Comment ça marche?* It is implied that Certeau's actor reconstructs a living object-relation in the memory of the father (*père*) engendering him with the mother (*mère*). A space of a primary scene stretches in the imagination between the *Rue des Saints-Pères* and the destination *chez sa mère*. The traumatic remembrance of an "inaugural rupture" that brought this pedestrian into the world is turned into a spatial trajectory in which there extends a desire to move ahead in time and space but, concomitantly, to return to the non-place of the individual's fabled origin. The trauma of separation and severance follows the itinerary of a promenade along the *Rue des Sèvres* from the man's home to the east and north, on a path to Paris, *de chez lui*. A habitus is invented by toponyms, on the printed page conveying the story, that emanate from the milieu, but also, simultaneously, by the active manipulation of names and forms that reach back into the common but secret spaces of psychogenesis. Certeau's friend retrieves the entire process of subjectivity, a fact and an experience that cannot be denied to *any* individual. In the narrative, the figure steers clear of the powers that would colonize the mind and body.

Here we discern a vital dimension of Certeau's approach to culture. A given area that is riddled with names, a determining surface of inscriptions similar to what is pregiven in the environment and the individual born into it, a bit like the zigzagged impressions riddling the clay surface of Freud's *Wunderbloc* described in his cryptic "Note on the 'Mystic Writing Pad,'" becomes the space in which takes place not a deadly scenario of repetition but a "creative swarm" (*un pullulement créateur*), where any number of poems can be written and forgotten in the same flash.[5] Pluralization of culture, it can be said here and throughout the author's political writings, begins with the early moments of psychomotor development. These moments are akin to what Certeau often, and both here and elsewhere, calls the *rupture inauguratrice* that every individual experiences and reinvents in coming into the world. The point is a fitting beginning for cultural studies, since the traumas of birth, growth, and death assure us that our relations with the world are built on things unknown.

Any pluralization of culture must be based on a respect and a tact that *welcome the unknown* through collective and singular experience. One of the most vital and common of all is our encounter of the world that we apprehend not only by moving backward, into the fiction we create of our past, but also forward, away and toward space that the body grasps without the symbolic threats or calming mediation of language. We often find ourselves born into "symbolic non-states" that elicit wonder, apprehension, and pleasure. When imposed as fact or unilateral law, a unilateral language of "culture" tends to eradicate the unknown that otherwise becomes the object of the arts of everyday life.

Readers familiar with Certeau's psychoanalytical writings quickly discover that his work on object relations also inflects his science of heterology, historiography, and his study of religion and mystical behavior. Crucial for these areas and for cultural studies is an article on Merleau-Ponty, titled "La folie de vision," in which he sketches out the itinerary that all of us take when we reinvent the world by mixing and confusing the signs—visual, sonorous, graphic, televisual, tactile—that bombard us from all directions.[6] The article theorizes what is related in the work on spatial practices. We become anonymous poets when we re-create a condition of protective and creative reception of symbolic signs. We turn what is supposed to be legible and audible into something *both* audible and visible, and vice versa, and therein we mime infancy by grasping bits of impressions that originate and are held in the secret spaces of our memories. We allow ourselves the chance to tap into a "lacunary reserve" of language that "goes mad" by virtue of our appropriation of its quasi-infinite possibility, but for ends that are critical for carving out creative arenas of culture.[7]

In *Culture in the Plural*, this sensibility is not set in bold type, but everywhere it informs the style of analysis. The process also informs the vision of *The Capture of Speech*, in the pages that build its politics from reflections on the psychogenesis of language in May 1968 in France (chapters 1–4). The revolts that shook the nation, argued the author, indicated that a deeply entrenched—at once political and historical—relation to language was resurfacing in the *way* that the insurgent students and workers used voluble speech for the purpose of staging an insurrection. But, alas, speech was and could only be spoken in the idiom of the dominant order. Whatever had to be stated about a very sorry lag between institutional standards and practices in the universities and the plight of students facing a dubious future (whose suspicions have since been confirmed by galloping unemployment) could only be expressed in a received language. Confined to inherited vocabularies and rhetorical procedures, dissidents unwittingly ratified what was scripted to be the collective perception of bratty recalcitrance. No ambience or subject-position was available to welcome expression of what could not yet be thought, what was *other* or *unknown* in the protests, what could be semanticized or, in the most ideal of worlds, elucidated. A natural "catch-22" occurred at a date seven years after the publication of Joseph Heller's novel of that title.

The spatial aspect of the insurrections supplanted what discourses could not convey, and in that way the utterances shared uncanny resemblances with what Certeau stated both about the man from Sèvres on the street of the Saintly Fathers and the possessed women of Loudun in the seventeenth century. The women could only skitter about or displace the vocabularies imposed on them when they were put on a stage and told to describe unnameable feelings. The dominant order told them what to say about the ineffable in the highly restrictive idiom it imposed. Official orders denied the women the experience of being born into a world of inherited shapes and forms; they also exorcised the women's creation of private discourses and spaces within their bodies. With the realization of the force of denial (in either seventeenth-century Loudun or in Paris in 1968) came an awareness of the way that power, far from being associated with a central organ such as a university or a French academy, was more pervasive in the organization of codes of speech.

Nothing in Certeau's psychogenetic reading of the revolts of 1968 resembled any of the pragmatism that marked anti-Vietnam protests led in North America. For Certeau, who had witnessed the growth of popular protest in America against the war in Vietnam, speech acquired dialogical traits by claiming "a 'symbolic place' designat[ing] the space created through the distance that separates the represented from their representations, the members of a society and the modalities of their association."[8] The only area that underscores the *lack* of a discourse of negotiation was located in the relation that the author disengaged from the dialogical world that, elsewhere, he had described through mystical practices in the sixteenth and seventeenth centuries.[9]

In this respect, several moments of *Culture in the Plural* are noteworthy. In the last chapter, Certeau coins the concept of a "French theater" to connote what exists in the psychogenetic areas of his work. The subjacent figures of the stage bears the aspect of a "diagram," a grid, or even a patrimonial map of France in the way it is taught to children in primary schools. It is also invested with what the clinical analyst Joyce McDougall calls the "theaters of the mind" and "theaters of the body" that frame our collective lives, and thus it evokes the painful but no less exhilarating process of separation that makes subjects aware of the pluricultural character of the physical world.[10] How does a subject grow into such a "theater" with its predetermined scenarios and preassigned roles? How to select an activity that will allow a creative life? The approach to an answer comes after the author decries the effects of a "pathological zone" of the "wasteland of culture" in which social tensions and ills are made manifest wherever we hear sanctimonious words about "man" and "values." In the contemporary national theater (*le théâtre français*), in the regime of media events, we need to see how people refuse to be assimilated into categories that define national identities or ideologies.

In France, people retract from the imposition of hexagonal order by going into exile.[11] They find "spaces in which they can get lost," taking refuge in the countryside, raising local consciousness, and the like, in order not to play the roles assigned to them on the national map.[12] "In gaining distance from the image, the public perceives through the conditions of its production. It evaluates the way it is made without going after its content." By sundering the effects of the media from the intentions seen through their expression, the public skitters about, avoiding wherever possible the hexagon and other identity traps placed everywhere in its midst. In the movement of retreat or displacement, the secret spaces of a people's lives, like that of the Parisian *promeneur* described earlier, are outlined. The spaces that are opened up, or in which subjects conceal themselves, serve first as a buffer, and then as a means to produce nonsymbolic conditions that resist commodification. It follows, Certeau remarks in many places, that the "cultural esperanto" of psychoanalysis has become more of a symptom of than a cure for the illness that economic imperialists have spread over the world. Even though psychogenesis serves to implement a consciousness in any politics of culture, the discipline in which it was born also risks composing a "new myth," a symptom of a state in which, wherever *more* jargons are made available to analyze cultural malaise, the *less* is spoken or even done to remedy the condition. In taking such a critical view of a lingua franca of French culture, Certeau keeps our relations with the unknown free of the normalizing effects of professional, scientific, and academic institutions.

It might be said that the means he uses to gain distance from images and media effects is based on an extensive history brought back, like the psychogenetic moment itself, into the conclusions about the need to pluralize our notions of culture. Two indications show why. First, when he speaks of the "French theater," he alludes to a diagram that, while it is supposed to classify or assign roles to subjects who live within its confines, remains an *arena* of silent but perpetual conflict. An art of culture is tantamount to finding ways of doing things that are not under the control of strategic forces. The figure is put forward to imply that we need to gain historical awareness of the inherited architectures that pattern everyday life. "Le théâtre français" also happens to designate the title of the first French atlases (1594–1632) that sought to plot out and unify the varied topographies of France into a graphic spectacle of the nation.[13] Those who tacitly refuse to be plotted on a national or cultural map with a deeply embedded history also refuse to be pigeonholed in schemes that are taken to be authentic representations of given places. By disinterring past representations that silently inhabit present expression, the student of culture reorients standard facts of history for political ends. The past is not used to establish a confirmation of the present, but as a form of displacement that mobilizes critical perspectives.

The point also informs the chapters on spatial narratives in *L'Invention du quotidien*. In the stroke of a couple of sentences, Certeau demonstrates that maps become autonomous machines that colonize the spaces they describe. In the speech we bring to them by way of interpretation, we reanimate them, we discover how they work in ways unbeknownst to themselves. We disinter and relocate them for ends other than their own. Apropos decorations and images on early modern maps, he remarks:

> Far from being "illustrations," iconic glosses of the text, these figurations, such as fragments of a narrative, inscribe upon the map the historical operations that give birth to it. Thus the sailboat painted on the sea is expressive of the maritime expedition that promoted the representation of the coastlines. It is equivalent to a "circuit"-like description. But the map progressively wins over these figures, colonizing the space, slowly eliminating the pictorial figurations of practices that give rise to it. Transformed by Euclidean, and then descriptive, geometry, constituted as a formal totality of abstract places, it becomes a "theater."[14]

He is saying that at a given stage of development in the representation of national space, a dialogue of textual and figural forms is silenced. Authority is gained when the coextension of visual and aural forms is sundered. It follows that the cartographical history that

Certeau sketches in describing the "theater" of France contains within its return to a dialogical condition of language a recipe for making or doing new things with the raw facts of a history of the description of space.

A pattern of analysis emerges: Certeau appeals to a past configuration on the threshold of the sixteenth and seventeenth centuries in order to change our perception of the griddings of quotidian reality of other times. In this instance, where locational imaging is used to control billions of subjects in our age, he shows that its effect of authority given by maps depends on the concealment of the history informing their design for control. A similar critical trajectory is plotted out in the brilliant chapter of *Culture in the Plural* titled "Culture and the Schools." In addressing sociocultural consequences of changes in the pedagogy of French language and literature in French secondary schools, Certeau broaches the issue of pluralization of the language in the world at large. *Other* forms of French return, like the unconscious, from beyond French borders, in decisive ways that invigorate the idiom. "Today, French is spoken in Canada, Belgium, Algeria, Morocco, sub-Saharan Africa, Libya, and so on. There are several kinds of French, not a unique or single French. The current plurality has to be part of its teaching if an analysis is to be proportioned to the linguistic experience of communication." The classroom, a miniature version of the "French theater," becomes a site where, contrary to the postrevolutionary mission that used a single language to unify the nation, different modes of speaking the idiom are deployed as so many practices. Extension of Francophone space outside of the fabled hexagon means "thinking French *in the plural*" and "introducing the relation with the other (Francophone or foreign French) as a necessary condition of learning and linguistic exchange."

At this point, right where the title of the book is located in the body of its text, a more extensive history of the practice of French is mentioned. With allusion to the other comes, simultaneously, a return of the past: Certeau notes how the authority of the nation was built on a French "frozen" (*gelé*) in printed books, and that the drive that sixteenth-century lexicographers launched to unify orthography also brought forward a unilateral view of etymology. With the fetishization of written language comes the Dictionary, "the arc de triomphe of written and past French, that of the 'authors' of yesteryear," which celebrates the "unknown" French that has never been spoken. Certeau admits that he stumbled upon this realization when he encountered American students who were abusing a tradition of French orthography that he himself had internalized. Their orthographic malapropisms (thank God for American stupidity!) reminded him of "my own history" by recalling the French writers of the sixteenth and seventeenth centuries who esteemed the fabulous variety of inflections in oral French over and above its limited expression in written form. He advocates our grasping the confusions of visual (graphic) and oral (spoken) uses of French that reinvent the idiom at a stage prior to any finalized mapping or codification in a French theater of cultural operations.

History, then, is part of the psychogenetic design of Certeau's approach to culture. What we can ascertain of the past by way of its animation in the present constitutes a way to "do something with something," to "change everyday reality" by conferring remote objects with a compelling—albeit almost indicible—voice that speaks to us across and through current images. A plan to pluralize culture therefore engages an existential relation with history, what might be called a reterritorialization, that leads simultaneously to creative complications and elucidations of quotidian experience. Insofar as media machines disguise the history of the signs they purvey, if cultural studies is to become a discipline endowed with political efficacity, it must tap into the defamiliarizing effects of informed historiography. In *The Writing of History,* Certeau compared it to the way that a proper name gains significance in literature. For the reader of *The Red and the Black,* "Julien Sorel" means little or nothing until an awareness is gained through Stendhal's narrative of the character's actions. Yet the historian, by contrast, begins with a household name, such as "Robespierre," and proceeds to estrange our received knowledge of it through archival labor and interpretation.[15]

The stakes are articulated in extraordinarily subtle ways in the penultimate chapter of *The Capture of Speech,* in which Certeau advocates a tactical use of history. A lost place of the past that would otherwise be given to mourning must be turned into an active space of fiction capable of being reinvented over and again. Such spaces are "fragments of rites, protocols of politeness, vestmental or culinary practices, codes of gift giving or of honor. They are odors, quotations of colors, explosions of sounds, tonalities." He calls these bits the "relics" detached from a lost social body. They acquire more force for us because they are *not* reintegrated in a new totality, for the reason that they can circulate from one body to another in the style of what, borrowing Freud's words, he calls "the little bits of truth" that the psychoanalyst located in the creative displacement of time-held traditions. Immigrants or *others* are best equipped to animate and mobilize these fragments. They make us accountable for consigning them to oblivion by dint of their own and different appropriations of what we believe is given or bequeathed to us.[16] They animate the spirits of a past, they "punctuate" the black spaces of our culture with new and different signs, or they confer new syntactic rhythms on inaudible or banal phrasings that circulate in the speech of our everyday lives. An "ethnic alterity" thus shares much with the deracinating effects of historical displacement. Facts bearing on the past, these "apparently trivial relics," have an irruptive power by concretizing what is misrepresented in the pedagogical grist of national histories. Therein the contents of knowledge are mistaken for truth when, in effect, the play of its signs constitutes an ongoing relation "with a dispersed patrimony."

What has been stated here is reflected prismatically in Certeau's other essays. In *Histoire et psychanalyse entre science et fiction* (much of which appears in English in *Heterologies*), history and psychoanalysis are configured as a mobile chiasmus that turns the one into the other in the same way that science and fiction become functions of each other's practices. Science, the discipline that proffers a troubled but inspired relation with its other, thrives on the mendacious practices of literature: as history elucidates more and more the polymorphous qualities of its relation with the past, it begins to resemble that of a subject traumatized by the forever "inaugural rupture" that gives rise to the re-creation of memories of object relations.[17]

For the sake of reclaiming culture studies in light of the experience of psychoanalysis, also noteworthy is the initial subhead of the first chapter of this volume: "Against Unconsciousness." Certeau contends that, in the wake of the revolution of communication effected in 1968, in the obtainment of the "right" to speech and its subsequent "recapture," a point was made that cannot be forgotten. In what was gained during the riots, a circuit of transference and recognition was established. Communities, he observes, found their bearings through "frames of reference" that did not need to obsess about clarity or perpetual illusions concerning an eternal day of reason and science that would otherwise be revived with revolutionary rhetoric.[18] A common experience, a swarming of culture, was ubiquitous. People needed to be given the right to be heard, and to speak in ways in which the symbolic content of their words was less important than their energetic expression.

In a congruent argument at the end of chapter 1 of *Culture in the Plural*, Certeau observes that in the labor of establishing social orders, there is a need "to reconstitute in common language, and through a critique of traditional stereotypes and powers that have become unthinkable, circuits that make a reciprocal recognition *possible*." In other words, he is not enslaving exchange to the democracy of common sense. A politics of exchange is initiated through a mystical inflection informing what he calls a "reciprocal recognition," a process by which an affirmation of an unstated condition of common being is affirmed before it happens to be named.[19] A community can live irrespective of the languages that controlling structures impose in order to produce conflict. A social cohesion lies elsewhere, in the unnameable areas where contradiction is felt outside of the languages typifying its limits and functions. Now we see how the psychogenetic model of subjectivity gives to the political dimension of the essays of this book a force and elegance of almost universal appeal.

In chapter 2, which seems anchored in debates about scopophilia that consumed film theory in the 1970s, Certeau takes the "imaginary" of the city to mean what fragments of its sum are seen less from a panoptic point of view than in the images in newspapers strewn about subway cars and gutters. Sight, he argues in a line that opposes the power of the gaze to the checks and balances of speech, is used by the mass media so that speech or the "reciprocal recognitions" of communication will be occluded. With speech come the same *inaugural ruptures* that Eros and love release in intimacy with subjective process. "The first communication, that of bodies in love, is at once an object of desire and an object of fear. With respect to the law, it does not conform." Hence the "denaturing" act of speech, hardly a sign of pure presence, becomes a useful affective tool that broadens the perspective of relations of identification.

The point is advanced in a different way in chapter 3. The act of *speaking* about violence (in question is the havoc wrought on Vietnam and Latin American nations by multinational capital) needs to be considered as a symptom of a system that exploits speech to neutralize awareness and thus to perpetuate violence beneath effects of consensus. Practices thus need to be built on the collective foundation of the knowledge of the general insignificance of meaning and content of speech so that action can supplant what, citing Artaud, Certeau calls the "impoverishment" of spoken words: conflict and struggle, understood in both a dialogical and a social sense, need to shatter "the anonymity of which language is but the symptom."

This dynamic view of communication grounds Parts II and III of the book, in which education and cultural politics are treated in commensurate terms. These chapters, although specific to the French national education policies of the 1970s, pertain to school as a means of obtaining critical views of culture. If, as we have seen, history is associated with the drama of awareness gained by separation from the idea of a nourishing origin, education becomes the welcoming field in which a cultural politics can gain a foothold. Schooling becomes a decisive space for the creation of a "multiplicity of cultural places," where "cultural porosities" and symbioses with places can be effected in order to soften and transform the frontiers of bodies in the pedagogical milieu. What is stated about minority cultures, student insurrection in the "social architecture" of knowledge, cultural studies as a "labor on the limits" of institutional forms, and the need to invest languages into the practice of culture follows the same lines of reasoning. In effect, the book is a virtual genesis of new and vital discipline.

The style of Certeau's writing in both *The Capture of Speech* and *Culture in the Plural* seems more direct and "spoken" than in his works on historiography or religion. Each essay makes a broad appeal through its analysis, effectively "inventing" its public through the tenor of its address. Given the compelling interlocutory manner of these essays, I have attempted to respect the direct and oral force of the French. A balance between an informal, engaged, popular diction and that of the archivist, the historian, and the sociologist has been sought. I have attempted to convey a sense of each essay as an unfinished labor that is shared with the reader. The preparation of both volumes has been facilitated by the work of Andrea Flores and the careful copyediting of David Thorstad. I would like to thank Luce Giard for suggesting that the project be undertaken, Richard Terdiman for timely suggestions about how to approach the translation, and Lisa Freeman for getting the work into print. The remaining blemishes and infelicities are the fault of the translator.

Notes

Preface

1. This chapter, titled "The Beauty of the Dead," appears in English in Michel de Certeau, *Heterologies: Discourse on the Other*, trans. Brian Massumi (Minneapolis: University of Minnesota Press, 1986), 119–36.

Introduction: Opening the Possible

1. The complete bibliography of the author, along with a collection of articles on his work is found in Luce Giard et al., *Le Voyage mystique. Michel de Certeau* (Paris: Cerf and Recherche de Science Religieuse, 1988). See also Luce Giard, ed., *Michel de Certeau* (Paris: Centre Georges-Pompidou, "Cahiers pour un temps," 1987); the dossier dedicated to him in *Le Débat*, no. 49 (March-April 1988); Luce Giard, Hervé Martin, and Jacques Revel, *Histoire, Mystique et Politique. Michel de Certeau* (Grenoble: Jérôme Millon, 1991); Claude Geffré, ed., *Michel de Certeau ou la différence chrétienne* (Paris: Cerf, "Cogitatio fidei," 1991); Luce Giard, "Michel de Certeau," in *Encyclopédie philosophique universelle*, vol. 3, *Les œuvres philosophiques*, ed. Jean-François Mattéi (Paris: PUF, 1992), 3112–113.

2. A new edition of *La prise de parole*, expanded to include other political writings, appeared in 1994 (Paris: Gallimard). [It is published as a companion volume to *Culture in the Plural.—Trans.*]

3. This chapter, titled "The Beauty of the Dead," appears in English in *Heterologies: Discourse on the Other*, trans. Brian Massumi (Minneapolis: University of Minnesota Press, 1986), 119–36.

4. On this theme, see the book Certeau coauthored with Dominique Julia and Jacques Revel, *Une politique de la langue: La Révolution française et les patois: l'enquête de Grégoire* (Paris: Gallimard, 1975).

5. This reference is to the chapter titled "The Beauty of the Dead," not included in this book. See note 3 above.—*Trans.*

6. On the Lip affair, which had extraordinary repercussions from 1973 to 1976, see Brigitte Camus-Lazaro, "Lip: les marches de l'utopie," *Le Monde*, June 13–14, 1993; Claude Neuschwander and Gaston Bordet, *Lip, vingt ans après* (Paris: Syros, 1993).

7. Marc Augé, "Présence, absence," in Giard, *Michel de Certeau*, 84.

8. Certeau's three books on culture can be arranged in a series: *La prise de parole* (1968; 1974) [*The Capture of Speech* (1997)], *La culture au pluriel* (1974) [*Culture in the Plural* (1997)], *L'Invention du quotidien* (1980; new edition 1990) [*The Practice of Everyday Life* (1984)]. It can be observed that this last work occupies an intermediary place in the chronology, as it does for the refinement of the concepts that will be keys to the vault of the most carefully designed work, that of 1980, which has been highly influential both in and outside of France. The crucial notions of *The Practice of Everyday Life*, such as the dyad of "strategy" and "tactic," or that of "operation," or yet again the recourse to a linguistics of enunciation—all these traits are already sketched out in the last chapters of the present book. This *Culture in the Plural* can legitimately serve as an introduction to Certeau's political anthropology, just as *L'Étranger ou l'Union dans la différence* (1969; new edition, Paris: Desclée de Brouwer, 1991) is an introduction to his history of mysticism and inner life.

Chapter 1. The Revolution of the "Believable"

1. By "authority" I mean everything that gives (or claims to give) reason to authority—representations or persons—and refers thus, in one way or another, to what is "received" as "believable."

2. Douaumont: tiny village taken and retaken by French and German troops in the battle of Verdun between February and September 1916, noted here to mean a senseless loss of life in a battle over a paltry bit of space. Viewers of cinema will recall Jean Renoir's equally ironic reference to Douaumont in *The Grand Illusion* (1937).— Trans.

3. No less frequent and formidable is the experience of incomprehension or confusion of "intellectuals" or authorities in view of a mass protest coming from depths about which they do not have the slightest inkling. See, for example, W. E. Mühlmann, *Messianismes révolutionnaires du tiers monde* (Paris: Gallimard, 1968), 271, 286, 347, 351, etc.; also, Michel de Certeau, *L'Absent de l'histoire* (Paris: Mame, 1973), chap. 6, 135–50.

4. *Journal d'un guérillero* (Paris: Seuil, 1968), 87, 110–12, etc.

5. Oscar Lewis, *The Children of Sanchez* (New York: Random House, 1961), 370.

6. Cf. Pierre Antoine, "Les surprises du moraliste," *Le Concours médical*, vol. 88, no. 43 (October 1966): 6427 ff.

7. Pierre-Joseph Proudhon, *Les Confessions d'un révolutionnaire* (Paris: Rivière, 1929), 57.

8. Edmund Husserl, *La Crise de l'humanité européenne et la philosophie* (1935), French translation by Paul Ricoeur (Paris: Aubier-Montaigne, 1977) of *Die Krisis der europäischen Wissenschaften und die transzendentale Phänomenologie*.

9. Cf. Michel de Certeau, *L'Étranger ou l'Union dans la différence*, 2d ed. (Paris: Desclée de Brouwer, 1991), chap. 5, 97–126.

10. M. Isaura Pereira de Queiroz, *Réforme et révolution dans les sociétés traditionnelles* (Paris: Anthropos, 1968), 260 (my emphasis); cf. also Certeau, *L'Absent de l'histoire*, chap. 6.

Chapter 2. The Imaginary of the City

1. See, for example, Georges Thill's analyses in *La Fête scientifique* (Paris: Aubier, "Bibliothèque des sciences religieuses," 1973), 156–81.

Chapter 3. The Language of Violence

1. G. W. F. Hegel, *The Phenomenology of Mind*, trans. J. D. Bailie. (repr. New York: Humanities, 1966) vol. 1, 2.1. French translation by Jean Hyppolite (Paris: Aubier, 1961), vol. 2, 71–84.

2. Cf. Jean Baudrillard, *Pour une critique de l'économie politique du signe* (Paris: Gallimard, 1972), 44–50. In English, *For a Critique of the Political Economy of the Sign*, trans. and introd. Charles Levin (Saint Louis, Mo.: Tellis Press, 1981).

3. Alexandre Passerin d'Entrèves, *La Notion de l'État* (Paris: Sirey, 1967). In English, *The Notion of the State* (Oxford: Clarendon Press, 1967).

4. Sigmund Freud, *Civilization and Its Discontents*, in *The Standard Edition of the Complete Psychological Works of Sigmund Freud*, vol. 21, trans. and ed. James Strachey (London: Hogarth Press, 1961), 89–97.

5. Cf. René Girard, *La violence et le sacré* (Paris: Grasset, 1972). In English, *Violence and the Sacred*, trans. Patrick Gregory (Baltimore: Johns Hopkins University Press, 1977).

6. Hannah Arendt, *Du mensonge à la violence* (Paris: Calmann-Lévy, 1972), 192.

7. Cf. Pierre Thuillier, *Jeux et enjeux de la science* (Paris: Robert Laffont, 1972), 298–329, or the publications by the Stockholm International Peace Research Institute (New York, 1971) and Robin Clarke, *La course à la mort* (Paris: Seuil, 1972). In English, *Science of War and Peace* (New York: McGraw-Hill, 1972).

8. Cf. Ignacy Sachs, *La Découverte du tiers monde* (Paris: Flammarion, 1971). In English, *The Discovery of the Third World*, trans. Michael Fineberg (Cambridge: MIT Press, 1976).

9. Maurice Merleau-Ponty, *Adventures of the Dialectic*, trans. Joseph Bien (Evanston, Ill.: Northwestern University Press, 1973), 27.

Chapter 4. Universities versus Popular Culture

1. See Michel de Certeau and Dominique Julia, "La misère de l'université," *Études* (April 1970): 522–44.

2. Cf. Antoine Proust, *L'Enseignement en France, 1800–1967* (Paris: Armand Colin, 1968).

3. René Kaës, *Images de la culture chez les ouvriers français* (Paris: Cujas, 1968), 156 (emphasis in the original).

4. See Jacques Dubois and Joseph Sumpf's remarkable "Analyse linguistique des rapports d'agrégation et du Capes," *Langue française* 5 (February 1970): 27–44.

5. Antoine Proust, "De quelques problèmes universitaires en France et aux États-Unis," *Esprit* (February 1970): 286–302.

6. From this point of view, the pedagogical implication within the university must be seen in light of problems of *method*. Today, *meaning* cannot be detached from a *practice*, nor knowledge from a reference to subjects who are familiar with its field of meaning. Such had been, for example, the meaning that Freud gave to the introduction of psychoanalysis in the teaching of medicine. Cf. "The Educational Interest of Psycho-Analysis," in *The Standard Edition of the Complete Psychological Works of Sigmund Freud*, vol. 13, trans. and ed. James Stachey (London: Hogarth Press, 1961), 189–90.

7. *Bulletin officiel de l'Éducation nationale* (March 26, 1970), 1094–1103.

8. Temporarily, perhaps, for, in the wake of a demand sent to Georges Pompidou (who closely followed the problem of medical training), the CHU may indeed be granted an autonomous status.

9. *Le Monde*, March 22–23, 1970, 15.

10. UER designated the credits (*unités*) of teaching and research defined by reference to a given discipline or group of disciplines [L. G.].

11. See Jacques Dubois and Joseph Sumpf, "Linguistique et pédagogie," in *Langue française* 5 (February 1970); Claude Philippe, *Note d'information concernant un cours de développement de la capacité de lecture donné à l'Institut universitaire de technologie de Montpellier* (June 1968); Edward Herbert Dance, *History the Betrayer: A Study in Bias* (London: Hutchinson, 1960); F. Lusset, "Une expérience de pédagogie vécue" (at Nanterre), *Allemagne aujourd'hui*, special issue (1970).

12. We can cite, as symptomatic of this, the reflection made by the Duke de Broglie, picked up by Montalembert in his speech of January 17, 1850, before the legislative Assembly: "The bachelor's diploma is a bill of exchange underwritten by society and must, soon or later, be paid through public service. If it is not paid off, in the worst scenario, we face this bodily constraint that is called a revolution" (Charles Forbes Montalembert, *œuvres*, vol. 3 [Paris: Lecoffre, 1860], 340).

13. Extreme cases have been shown, first, with the "manual" laborer for whom language is an instrument of expression, a point of reference, indeed, a way of acquiring a better position, and, second, with the "intellectual" laborer who turns language into his or her milieu and raw material. Between these extreme cases extends a whole series of positions. Key is that the *relationship to language* and, if one prefers, the instrumentality of language are called into question, and that their homogeneity inside of a scholarly discipline or in the totality of society at large can no longer be counted on.

14. Cf., for example, Yvette Desaut's analysis, "Les opinions politiques dans le système des attitudes: les étudiants en lettres et la politique," *Revue française de sociologie* 11 (1970): 45–64. That does not mean, as the author seems to believe, that these political discourses are not to be taken seriously. Through another sort of illusion, she supposes that in order to have other meanings the discourse no longer has what it affirms. Under the pretext of psychologizing or of sociologizing, it can be said that this simplification means the suppression of cultural ambiguity and heterogeneity.

15. Cf. F. Bourricaud, "Le kaléidoscope universitaire," *Projet* (September 1968): 920–35.

16. In "Chahut traditionnel et chahut anomique dans l'enseignement du second degré," *Revue française de sociologie* 8 (special issue) (1967): 17–33, Jean Testanière shows how the appearance of a new kind of uproar is linked to social mobility and diversification of the student public. From this relation between the expansion of this public and the diminution of its aptitude to be integrated in the traditional pedagogical system, the implications and the cultural manifestations remain to be evaluated.

17. Alfred Willener analyzes diverse forms of this phenomenon in *L'Image-action de la société ou la politisation culturelle* (Paris: Seuil, 1970). In English, *The Action-Image of Society: On Cultural Politicization*, trans. A. M. Sheridan-Smith (New York: Pantheon Books, 1971).

18. On this topic, it should be emphasized how intolerable the culture is that combines the impossibility of taking action with the accumulation of knowledge. Studies on primary education have shown how increased information on the misfortunes

of Biafra or the Vietnam War traumatized children, when the information was accompanied by a demystification of forms of assistance that, formerly, proportioned *activities* to *forms of knowledge*. We can recall the student from Lille who asked, the day before he immolated himself, "Can a form of action still be envisioned?" The question is universal. Violence is a symptom more than a response.

19. On the IUT, a decisive problem, the first studies devoted to them after their creation (January 7, 1966) can be consulted: R. Guillemoteau and G. Salesse, "Les Instituts universitaires de technologie," *Éducation*, no. 8 (November 7, 1968); A. Leblond, "La place des IUT dans l'enseignement supérieur," *Avenirs*, no. 188 (November 1967): 46–50; M. Menard, "Les IUT," *Avenirs*, no. 189 (December 1967); F. Russo, "Les IUT," *Études*, (July-August 1967); *Le Monde*, June 10, 1970, and so on.

20. Certeau and Julia, "La Misère de l'université," 525.

21. Paul Ricoeur, letter of resignation, printed in *Le Monde*, March 18, 1970.

22. On this topic, see the studies of Pierre Bourdieu and Jean-Claude Passeron, *La Reproduction* (Paris: Minuit, 1970). In English, *Education, Society and Culture*, trans. Richard Nice with a foreword by Richard Bottomore (Beverly Hills, Calif.: Sage, 1977).

23. Ernest Bloch-Lainé, "Bâtir des utopies concrètes," *Projet* (May 1970): 513.

24. J. Julliard, "Sauver l'université," *Le Nouvel Observateur*, May 4–10, 1970.

Chapter 5. Culture and the Schools

1. Marcel Rouchette, ed., *Vers un enseignement rénové de la langue française à l'école élémentaire* (Paris: Armand Colin, 1969) [L. G.].

2. In saying that, I do not wish to neglect the necessity of the dictionary; nor am I forgetting the marvel and jubilation inspired by itineraries through the alphabetical corridors of the Littré or the Robert, which tell of the travels, the metamorphoses, and the resources of words. But these (quasi-professional) pleasures of writing must not be confused with the contracts of the spoken language.

3. Fachoda: area in the Egyptian Sudan visited by the French Marchand mission in 1898 that was soon conceded to the British. The site is taken to mean a sorry moment in nineteenth-century colonial history.—*Trans.*

Chapter 6. Minorities

1. Remarks edited in 1972 by Patrick Mignon and Olivier Mongin.

2. Larzac, "Décoloniser l'histoire occitane," *Les Temps modernes* (November 1971).

3. Edgar Morin, *Commune en France: la métamorphose de Plodémet* (Paris: Fayard, 1967). In English, *The Red and the White: Report from a French Village*, trans. A. M. Sheridan-Smith (New York: Pantheon Books, 1970).

Chapter 7. The Social Architecture of Knowledge

1. See Michel de Certeau, *The Capture of Speech and Other Political Writings*, ed. and introd. Luce Giard, trans. and Afterword Tom Conley (Minneapolis: University of Minnesota Press, 1997), chap. 5.

2. To finally make *true* statements was what was asked through so many accusations leveled against the "lies" of institutions. But Julien Freund argued, even recently,

that "sincerity is a private, not a public, virtue" (in *L'Essence du politique* [Paris: Sirey, 1965], 161; cf. 199). However, even if they are utopian (in part because they are born outside of the sites of political responsibility), these demands at the very least attest to a displacement of *ethical* conscience, which has henceforth become a *political* requirement. The restoration or the innovation of a "truth" of representations and communications must correspond to the suspicion that bores into "values" invested in social exchanges.

3. Cf. Andrew Schonfield, *Modern Capitalism: The Changing Balance of Public and Private Power* (New York and London: Oxford University Press, 1965), 71–87.

4. Cf. Robert K. Merton, *Social Theory and Social Structure* (Glencoe, Ill.: Free Press, 1949), 120–52.

5. That is clearly what Robert Mandrou himself "states" in his inventory of the "bibliothèque bleue" of Troyes, a collection of popular editions sold by itinerant merchants in eighteenth-century France (*De la culture populaire aux XVIIe et XVIIIe siècles* [Paris: Stock, 1964]). There are, unfortunately, few equivalents of this exemplary work. Nonetheless, its conclusions, or rather its assumptions, seem debatable. Robert Montrou betrays why: the booklets edited in Troyes draw off older material and simplify conceptions that reach back to the sciences of astrology or medicine in the sixteenth century. But can we conclude that they show us the rural culture in which they are diffused? They represent a *leftover* of elite culture, and this leftover is exactly what the authors ("squires," theologians, etc.) and the editors of Troyes *produce for the use* of the villagers and what they sell to them. It is a commercial production that "trickles down" from the learned class to people through the intermediary of these local printers and that attests, rather, to the conception that the *manufacturers* make for popular culture. That the literature is sold and read does not prove that it renders an account of the language of the rural people of the period. It might prove that they lived outside of the "literary" circles, from whose tables the crumbs fell into their midst. Geneviève Bollème notes, furthermore: "Made for the people, this literature nonetheless speaks neither of it nor for it. The people are absent from these works that are intended to be written for it" and by specialists ("Littérature populaire et littérature de colportage au XVIIIe siècle," in *Livre et Société dans la France du XVIIIe siècle* [The Hague: Mouton, 1965], 66–67). Similarly, would it now be a worthwhile method to assimilate the culture of television viewers to the tenor of the programs aimed at them? It would mean confusing the expression of a local (and no doubt *different*) experience for the cultural system that is imposed on it from above and that tends either to eliminate or to marginalize it further. Here too, up to the analysis of a "popular culture," the intellectual paradigm of an elite *postulates* in advance the result that will justify it. The fact is all the more noteworthy in that the book is remarkable.

6. I especially refer to the very nuanced report by Pierre Vilar, "Enseignement primaire et culture populaire sous la IIIe République," in *Niveaux de culture et groupes sociaux* (The Hague: Mouton, 1968), 267–76.

7. See in particular Pierre Bourdieu and Jean-Claude Passeron, *Les Héritiers*, rev. ed. (Paris: Minuit, 1966); Pierre Bourdieu, "La transmission de l'héritage culturel," in *Darras. Le partage des bénéfices* (Paris: Minuit, 1966), 387–405; and Pierre Bourdieu, "L'École conservatrice. Les inégalités devant l'École et devant la culture," *Revue française de sociologie* 6 (1966): 325–47. From a methodological point of view, Pierre Bourdieu has pointed out the danger among sociologists of a certain "class ethnocentrism":

"Among all the cultural presuppositions in which researchers risk engaging in their interpretations, the 'ethos' of class, a principle on which the acquisition of other unconscious models are organized, acts in the most systematic and obsequious of ways" (Pierre Bourdieu, Jean-Claude Chamboredon, and Jean-Claude Passeron, *Le Métier de sociologue*, [Paris: Mouton-Bordas, 1968], 108, a page that should be cited in entirety).

8. Oscar Lewis, *Pedro Martinez: A Mexican Peasant and His Family* (New York: Random House, 1964).

9. Philippe Ariès, *L'Enfant et la Vie familiale sous l'Ancien Régime* (Paris: Plon, 1960).

10. On this topic, see Henri Lefebvre, *Introduction à la modernité* (Paris: Minuit, 1962), 159–68.

11. Michel de Certeau, *L'Étranger ou l'Union dans la différence*, 2d ed. (Paris: Desclée de Brouwer, 1991), chap. 3.

12. *L'Archibras*, no. 4 (no series), "Le surréalisme le 18 juin 68": 2.

13. In a lucid and vigorous report in which he emphasized "the right to produce culture or the right that is granted to a social group (possibly to every individual) of playing an active role in the community," Giulio Carlo Argan protested against "the idea of a monocentric culture with a periphery organized around a radiating core." Our technological culture, he added, "is only the most current and, perhaps, terminal phase of a cultural phenomenon that, since the eighteenth century, has been strictly tied to the European and American history of thought, politics, and economy"; it is not "universal" (Report for the "Meeting of Experts on Cultural Rights as Human Rights," UNESCO, Paris, July 8–13, 1968).

14. See especially the three latest works of Herbert Marcuse, *Soviet Marxism: A Critical Analysis* (London: Routledge and Kegan Paul, 1969), *Eros and Civilization: Philosophical Inquiry into Freud*, with a new preface by the author (Boston: Beacon Press, 1966), *One Dimensional Man: Studies in the Ideology of Advanced Industrial Societies* (Boston: Beacon Press, 1966).

15. Martin Heidegger, *Questions III* (Paris: Gallimard, 1955).

16. Herbert Marcuse, "Critique of Neo-Freudian Revisionism," in *Eros and Civilization*, 207–36.

17. Strongly marked by the failure of the revolution in Germany (1918), along with Georges Lukács and Karl Morsch, Marcuse was one of the thinkers of what has been called the "Dialectical School of European Marxism." Beginning in 1934, he taught at Columbia University, where his interests turned increasingly toward Freudian aesthetics and psychology.

18. In fact, one has to look elsewhere than in Marcuse for a serious presentation of socioeconomic structures. Thus, preferable to the Marcusian legend of the "consumer society" (however tempting it may be) is John Kenneth Galbraith's analysis of "technostructure" in *The New Industrial State* (Boston: Houghton Mifflin, 1967), 60–71. The study that Galbraith makes of relations between the "educational and scientific estate" (282–316) and the technostructure moreover underlines the conflicts and is inspired by theses contrary to those of Marcuse.

19. See Pierre Bourdieu and Jean-Claude Passeron, "L'examen d'une illusion," *Revue française de sociologie* 2, special issue on 1968 ("Sociologie de l'éducation"): 227–53.

20. Cf. René Kaës, *Les ouvriers français et la culture* (Paris; Dalloz, 1962); Paul-Marie de La Gorce, *La France pauvre* (Paris: Grasset, 1965); Michael Harrington, *L'autre*

Amérique (Paris: Gallimard, 1967); and Jules Klanfer, *Le sous-développement humain* (Paris: Éditions Ouvrières, 1967), to cite only the most accessible titles. All of the conclusions tend to restore as a datum of *culture* this reality at once marginalized and fundamental that Oscar Lewis called "the culture or subculture of poverty" (*The Children of Sanchez* [New York: Random House, 1961], xxv) or the "culture de l'appauvrissement" (*Économie et humanisme*, no. 174 [May–June 1967]: 77–81).

21. André Glucksmann, *Stratégie et révolution en France: 1968* (Paris: Christian Bourgois, 1968), 80.

22. That is exacly what Michel Foucault recently recalled in the first part of his "Réponse à une question" (*Esprit*, May 1968, 850–74).

Chapter 8. Culture within Society

1. Ota Klein, "Révolution scientifique et technique et style de vie," *L'Homme et la Société*, no. 9 (1968): 14.

2. Stefan Zolkiewski, "Le plan de consommation et le modèle de culture," *Analyse et prévision* 3 (1967): 346–52. Based on a Polish model, this study shows how cultural problems emerge in a socialist economic regime.

3. On the "counterculture," see the classic work of Theodore Roszak, *Vers une contre-culture* (Paris: Stock, 1970). In English, *The Making of the Counterculture: Reflexions on the Technocratic Society and Its Youthful Opposition* (repr. Berkeley: University of California Press, 1995).

4. See Radovan Richta, *La Civilisation au carrefour* (Paris: Anthropos, 1969), 1–87. In English, *Civilisation at the Crossroads: Social and Human Implications of the Scientific and Technological Revolution*, trans. Marian Slingova (White Plains, N.Y.: International Arts and Science Press, 1969).

5. The basic study of the society of spectacle is Raoul Vaneigem, *Traité de savoir-vivre à l'usage des jeunes générations* (Paris: Gallimard, 1967). Partially in English as *Treatise on Living for the Youths of the Young Generation* (New York: Situationist International, 1970).

6. The Fourth French Plan (1962–65) introduced the expression "cultural planning," a term more exact than that of "cultural politics," to designate the nature of research led by the Ministry of Cultural Affairs since its creation in 1959. See *Aspect de la «politique culturelle» française* (UNESCO, 1970), 9–20. Edgar Morin has produced the best analysis of the theme in "De la culturanalyse à la politique culturelle," *Communications*, no. 14 (1969): 5–38.

7. See Pierre Bourdieu and Jean-Claude Passeron, *La Reproduction* (Paris: Minuit, 1970). In English, *Reproduction in Education, Society and Culture*, trans. Richard Nice, introd. Tom Bottomore (Beverly Hills, Calif.: Sage, 1977).

8. Clearly, social stratification that is eradicated by the homogeneous discourse of the mass media plays an important role in the sifting of information and in the differentiation of interpretation. See Maurice Flamant, "Information et stratification sociale," *Analyse et prévision* 13.1 (1972): 1–18. But it is then *concealed* in the reception of messages, less and less perceptible on the surface of language, deprived of objective points of reference.

9. On the structure of labor unions and workers' representations, see Gérard Adam and others, *L'Ouvrier français en 1970* (Paris: Armand Colin, 1970), 15–60.

10. Already in 1965, Paul Lazarsfeld noted that the retraction of culture and class consciousness among workers was caused by mass culture ("Les intellectuels et la culture de masse," *Communications*, no. 5 [1965]: 11–12). For France, the basic study is René Kaës, *Images de la culture chez les ouvriers français* (Paris: Cujas, 1968).

11. See André Régnier, "Les surprises de l'idéologie. Lutte des classes et technocratie," *L'Homme et la Société*, no. 20 (1971): 157–62.

12. A broad clientele buys paperbacks or continues to subscribe to encyclopedias or to take correspondence courses without being able to read or follow them, simply because of a lack of supporting structures, progressive initiation into the material, and meetings.

Chapter 9. The Place from Which One Deals with Culture

1. This chapter is the transcription of a lecture inaugurating a European symposium on the topic "Prospectives for Cultural Development" (Arc-et-Senans, April 1972), for which Michel de Certeau was the principal moderator [L. G.].

2. The Arc-et-Senans colloquium took place in preparation for the meeting of the ministers of cultural affairs in Helsinki in July 1972.

3. The author refers to the work of the Tavistock Institute of Human Behavior, which includes Russell L. Ackoff, *A Concept in Corporate Planning* (New York: Wiley-Interscience, 1970); Frederick E. Emery, *Form and Content in Industrial Democracy: Some Experiences from Norway and Other European Countries* (London: Tavistock, 1969) and *Towards a Social Sociology: Contextual Appreciations of the Future in the Present* (New York: Plenum, 1975); Eric Trist and Hugh Murray, eds., *The Social Engagement of Social Science: A Tavistock Anthology* (Philadelphia: University of Pennsylvania Press, 1990); Eric Trist et al., *Organizational Choice: Capabilities of Groups at the Coal Face under Changing Technologies* (London: Tavistock, 1963). — *Trans.*

4. Certeau is referring to the SIPRI (Stockholm International Peace Research Institute) series of monographs on international law, chemical warfare, disarmament, and world politics. The titles are published on a worldwide basis. — *Trans.*

5. On Ivan Illich's strange itinerary, see Michel de Certeau, "Cuernavaca: le centre interculturel et Mgr Illich," *Études* 331 (October 1969): 436–40 [L. G.].

Chapter 10. Conclusion: Spaces and Practices

1. The relation between a mapped *representation* and the ulterior *practice* of urban space is a problem that most studies of new cities consider but never solve. Cf. *Runcorn New Town Master Plan* (Runcorn, England: Runcorn Development Corp., 1966); *The Plan for Milton Keynes* (Bletchley, England: Milton Keynes Development Corporation, 1970), etc. For Charles Alexander, the "natural" city is a totality of systems superimposed on each other, irreducible to a single model; a "trellis" system has to be envisaged (*De la synthèse de la forme* [Paris: Dunod, 1971] and "Une ville n'est pas un arbre," *Architecture aujourd'hui* [1969]). But this plurality of systems is found in the actual functioning of the "artificial" city itself.

2. Hence the reactions of the "public," which increasingly practices abstention in political matters and intervenes when economic questions are posed. This is a general phenomenon. See Albert O. Hirschman, *Exit, Voice and Loyalty* (Cambridge: Harvard University Press, 1970).

3. In 1954 the bookseller Pierre Poujade launched a program aimed at protecting small businesses in France; his protests against the national tax system conveyed the conservative nature of his philosophy. — *Trans.*

4. This general problem is reproduced by another, which concerns the *representation* of given facts: the result of a statistical analysis is structured by the variable that is sought to be headlined; it is the product and the reflection of a constructive operation, whereas it is assumed to be stating "what is real." See Hervé Le Bras, "La Mortalité actuelle en Europe. Présentation et représentation des données," *Population* 27 (1972): 271–93.

5. It would thus seem necessary to introduce statistical or sociological "representation" into the analysis of the "society of spectacle" as Raoul Vaneigem inaugurated it in his *Traité de savoir-vivre* (Paris: Gallimard, 1967) and according to the methods that Erving Goffman uses with respect to daily life in *The Presentation of Self in Everyday Life* (Woodstock, N.Y.: Overlook Press, 1973).

6. Serge Moscovici already foresaw the problem in *La Psychanalyse, son image et son public* (Paris: PUF, 1961).

7. Oscar Lewis, *The Children of Sanchez* (New York: Random House, 1961); Miguel Barnet, *Esclave à Cuba* (Paris: Gallimard, 1967); Jan Myrdal, *Un village de la Chine populaire* (Paris: Gallimard, 1972).

8. James Agee and Walker Evans, *Let Us Now Praise Famous Men* (Boston: Houghton Mifflin, 1941).

9. Cf. Alfred Willener's analyses in *L'Image-action de la société* (Paris: Seuil, 1970), and those of Paul Beaud and A. Willener in *Musique et vie quotidienne* (Paris: Mame, 1973).

10. See especially *Langages* 17 (1970), devoted to the topic of enunciation.

11. On the Fiat strike of 1969–70 and its context, see *Il Manifesto* (Paris: Seuil, 1971), 99–150. On the Lip struggle, see Edmond Maire et al., in *Lip 73* (Paris: Seuil, 1973); Charles Piaget, *Lip* (Paris: Lutter-Stock, 1973).

12. The city as *an object of a reading practice* has already been taken up in the recent works of Kevin Lynch (*L'Image de la ville* [Paris: Dunod, 1969]) and Claude Sousy (*L'Image du centre dans quatre romans contemporains* [Paris: Centre de Sociologie Urbaine, 1971], especially the first part). But to this imaginary practice of the city are only beginning to be added actual practices, the ways in which a city, streets, squares, and so on, are used. See Manuel Castells, *The Urban Question* (London: Arnold, 1977).

13. Carlos Castañeda, *The Teachings of Don Juan: A Yaqui Way of Knowledge* (New York: Ballantine, 1968), 82.

Afterword: A Creative Swarm

1. See the last paragraph of Luce Giard's Introduction, "Opening the Possible," which notes the original dates and places of publication. Chapter 3 of *La culture au pluriel*, "The Beauty of the Dead: The Concept of 'Popular Culture,'" has been omitted from this edition. It is included in *Heterologies: Discourse on the Other*, trans. Brian Massumi (Minneapolis: University of Minnesota Press, 1986), 119–36. Readers wishing to see how Michel de Certeau establishes a history of the concept of "popular culture" can refer to this essay, which plays a vital role in the overall design.

2. By this division is meant the "First" and "Third" Worlds that generally define the arena of decolonization at large. The "Second" World is imagined whenever "balkanization" is invoked to call into question the atavistic appeal to integral communities

based on myth. It includes the Eastern European bloc and the Soviet Union after its collapse but can refer to any number of areas that witness regression to designs of national integration. The Fourth World is, of course, the zones in which new classes of pariahs live in all of the other worlds, whether in the urban peripheries (as about Paris) or elsewhere. *Culture in the Plural* will probably appear to most readers as one of the most precocious works among many that have studied redistribution of space. These also include Marc Augé, *Non-Spaces: Introduction to an Anthropology of Supermodernity*, trans. John Howe (London: Verso, 1995); Tim Cresswell, *In Place/Out of Place: Geography, Ideology, and Transgression* (Minneapolis: University of Minnesota Press, 1996); Rajagopalan Radhakrishnan, *Diasporic Mediations: Between Home and Location* (Minneapolis: University of Minnesota Press, 1996).

3. The English title does not carry the sense of "invention" resonant in the French, *L'Invention du quotidien*. Because of its roots in *invenire*, meaning an act of choice or selection, of letting happen what happens, the idea of "practice" is aligned with the performative world of classical rhetoric, in which topics and places are infused with the force of speech. For Certeau, invention does not begin ex nihilo, but comes from a set of practical choices.

4. Michel de Certeau, *L'Invention du quotidien*, vol. 1, *Arts de faire*, ed. Luce Giard (Paris: Gallimard, "Folio," 1990), 174; my translation).

5. Sigmund Freud,"A Note on the 'Mystic Writing Pad' " (1925), in *The Standard Edition of the Complete Psychological Works of Sigmund Freud*, vol. 19, trans. and ed. James Strachey (London: Hogarth Press, 1961), 227–34.

6. Michel de Certeau, "La folie de vision," first published in *Esprit* (in a special issue on Merleau-Ponty, especially *The Visible and the Invisible* [June 1982]: 85–99); translated into English by Michael B. Smith as "The Madness of Vision," *Enclitic* 7.1 (1983): 24–31. The nearest equivalent in English to the grain of Certeau's psychogenetic writings is probably Gabriele Schwab, in two decisive chapters in *The Mirror and the Killer-Queen: Otherness in Literary Language* (Bloomington: Indiana University Press, 1996). In a chapter on Marguerite Duras, she draws on Christopher Bollas's concept of the "unthought known," in which "unconscious memories of very early stages of being and relating before the acquisitions of language and object-formation" are vital to the advent of sensibility. She calls this a "nonsymbolic self-state" (180) that typifies the condition of love in Duras's writings. In a study of witchcraft and Hawthorne's *The Scarlet Letter*, she shows how the heroine of the story succeeds in *resemanticizing* inherited and imposed languages of repression in ways that recoup Certeau's work on the witchcraft trials in seventeenth-century Loudun (in *The Writing of History* [New York: Columbia University Press, 1992], chap. 6). For this and other references to Michel de Certeau's bibliography, see Luce Giard, "Bibliographie complète de Michel de Certeau," in Luce Giard et al., *Le Voyage mystique. Michel de Certeau* (Paris: Cerf and Recherche de Science Religieuse, 1988): 191–243. The list contains 419 entries plus citation of 146 shorter articles and reviews.

7. Michel Foucault uses "lacunary reserve" to designate the endless possibility of alteration and distortion contained in the language of everyday life, in "La folie, absence de l'œuvre" (first published in 1964), in Daniel Defert and François Ewald, eds., Michel Foucault, *Dits et écrits*, vol. 1, *1954–1969* (Paris: Gallimard, 1994), 412–20.

8. Michel de Certeau, *The Capture of Speech and Other Political Writings*, trans. Tom Conley (Minneapolis: University of Minnesota Press, 1997), 9.

9. This observation requires refinement. In *Une politique de la langue: La Révolution française et les patois: l'enquête de Grégoire* (Paris: Gallimard, 1975), one of the most brilliant but overlooked works of psychohistoriography coauthored with Dominique Julia and Jacques Revel, Certeau shows that the same modalities—the imposition of a natural language, like a received cartography—served to impose the idea of a culture and a savage state. The latter obtained its denomination by being unable to speak the language impressed upon it by the French colonizers of France. At stake was a simple poll led by the Abbé Grégoire about the status of French and dialects spoken in the countryside.

10. Joyce McDougall, *Theaters of the Body: A Psychosomatic Approach to Psychosomatic Illness* (New York: Norton, 1989); and Joyce McDougall, *Theaters of the Mind: Illusion and Truth on the Psychoanalytic Stage* (New York: Brunner/Mazel, 1991) (originally in French as *Théâtres du je* [1982]).

11. Noteworthy is that the very idea of France as a hexagonal shape is a fact of history. Christian Jacob (in *L'empire des cartes* [Paris: Albin Michel, 1992]) reminds us that Italy resembled a high-heeled boot only after 1840, when a comparison was possible because of the advent of new styles of footwear. Only in the years 1950–60 is France characterized as a hexagon, when the metaphor appears in dictionaries and encyclopedias (186). Jacob adroitly adds, in a certellian vein, "in its geometrical perfection, the hexagonal logo is frequently used by agencies of territorial planning, ministries, and political parties, but also insurance companies and large national causes; it has become an instrument of communication, indeed, of marketing" (440–41).

12. In a study of the mystical properties of Hieronymus Bosch's *Garden of Earthly Delights,* Certeau argues that the landscape of forms and of languages offers to the spectator a rare "place in which to get lost" (in *The Mystic Fable,* trans. Michael B. Smith [Chicago: University of Chicago Press, 1992], chap. 2). The drift of the argument bears analogy with the cultural politics of withdrawal in these pages of *Culture in the Plural.*

13. *Le théâtre françoys* is elegantly studied by Père François de Dainville, in "Le premier atlas de France: *Le théâtre françoys* de M. Bouguereau, 1594," in *Comité de travaux historiques et scientifiques: Actes du 85ᵉ congrès national des sociétés savantes, Chambéry-Annecy 1960, Section de Géographie* (Paris: Bibliothèque Nationale, 1961), and in "L'évolution de l'atlas de France sous Louis XIII: *Théâtre géographique du royaume de France des Le Clerc, 1619–32,*" (Paris: Bibliothèque Nationale, 1962), 1–51. In *The Self-Made Map: Cartographic Writing in Early Modern France* (Minneapolis: University of Minnesota Press, 1996), I attempt to show how a "nation" is conveyed through an unconscious assemblage of maps drawn in a graphic style *foreign* to the nation (245–47).

14. *L'Invention du quotidien,* 178; my translation.

15. Michel de Certeau, *The Writing of History,* trans. Tom Conley (New York: Columbia University Press, 1992), 82.

16. Unlike a code of honor, a tradition, Freud notes, amounts to "incomplete and blurred memories" of the past (*Moses and Monotheism,* the last part of I[B], "Latency Period and Tradition," in *The Standard Edition,* vol. 23, 71).

17. See Malcolm Bowie, *Freud, Proust, and Lacan: Fiction as Theory and Theory as Fiction* (Cambridge: Cambridge University Press, 1987).

18. Such is the topic of Jean Starobinski's *Les emblèmes de la raison* (Geneva: Skira, 1973), many of whose points about the paradox of eternal light and illumination are studied through Freud's distrust of the Aufklärung in chapter 9 of *The Writing of History.*

19. Certeau makes the same point in a different register in "The Gaze: Nicholas of Cusa," *Diacritics* 7.3 (fall 1987), in which our aural gaze is shared by a social body without any of its members needing to acknowledge its presence: "The experience of the gaze consists in believing without seeing, thus in living in society, in 'understanding each other'" (19). What is said can be compared to Gilles Deleuze, apropos the issue of a Baroque point of view that deals not with relativism (which would be democratic or commonsensical), "not a variation of truth according to the subject, but the condition in which the truth of a variation appears to the subject" in a collective process (*The Fold: Leibniz and the Baroque,* trans. Tom Conley [Minneapolis: University of Minnesota Press, 1993], 207).

Index

Ackoff, Russell L., 125, 171n3
Adam, Gérard, 170n9
Agee, James, 138, 172n8
Alexander, Charles, 171n1
Antoine, Pierre, 164n6
Arc-et-Senans Conference on Cultural
    Development, 123–32, 171nn1,2
Arendt, Hannah, 165n6
Argan, Carlo Giulio, 169n13
Ariès, Philippe, 88, 169n9
Artaud, Antonin, 31, 161
Astérix, 110
Augé, Marc, 163n7, 173n2
Austin, James Lloyd, 29
authority, 164n1; as affiliation, 13;
    as what listens, 12–13; and culture,
    3–4, 6, 9
automation, and labor, 105
autonomy (political), 78 (Algeria);
    69–79, 150 (Brittany)

Balandier, Georges, 129
Barnet, Miguel, 172n7
Baudrillard, Jean, 165n2
Beaud, Paul, 172n9
blasphemy, 34; and the French schools,
    49
Bloch-Lainé, Ernest, 52, 167n22
Bollas, Christopher, 173n6
Bollème, Geneviève, 168n5
Bordet, Gaston, 163n6
Borges, Jorge Luis, 18

Bosch, Hieronymus, 174n12
Bouguereau, Maurice, 174n13
Bourdieu, Pierre, 86, 98, 127, 167n22,
    168–69n7; and Jean-Claude Passeron,
    169n19, 170n7
Bourricaud, F., 166n15
Bowie, Malcolm, 174n17
Brecht, Bertolt, 53
Brothers, Dr. Joyce, 110

Camus-Lazaro, Brigitte, 163n6
Castañeda, Carlos, 172n13
Castells, Manuel, 172n12
centralized education in France, 44, 58,
    59, 62, 64, 84, 86
Certeau, Michel de, vii; and anti-
    Vietnam protests, 154; approach
    to culture, ix–xiv; bibliography of
    works, 163n1, 173n6; and education,
    161; and French "national theater,"
    155–56; and historiography, 157–58;
    location of *Culture in the Plural* in
    writings, 164n8; and Maurice
    Merleau-Ponty, 153, 173n6; and May
    1968, xi–xiii, 153; as moderator of
    Arc-et-Senans conference (1972),
    171n2; and politics, xiv; and
    psychogenesis, 151–52, 159; and
    violence, xiii; *L'Absent de l'histoire*,
    164nn2,3; *The Capture of Speech and
    Other Political Writings*, x, 149, 153,
    158, 163n2, 167n1, 164n8, 173n8;

Before his untimely death in 1986, Michel de Certeau had authored numerous articles and books, including *The Writing of History, The Mystic Fable, The Practice of Everyday Life, The Stranger: Union in Difference,* and *Heterologies: Discourse on the Other* (1986, University of Minnesota Press). A historian of religion and a student of ethnography, Michel de Certeau was a professor at both the École des Hautes Études en Sciences Sociales, Paris, and the University of California, San Diego. The second volume of his *Practice of Everyday Life,* coauthored with Luce Giard and Pierre Mayol, is forthcoming from the University of Minnesota Press.

Tom Conley is professor of French at Harvard University. He is the translator of *The Writing of History* by Michel de Certeau, *The Fold* by Gilles Deleuze, and *The Year of Passages* by Reda Bensmaïa. Conley is also the author of *Film Hieroglyphs* (1991) and *The Self-Made Map: Cartographic Writing in Early Modern France* (1996), both published by the University of Minnesota Press.

Luce Giard is a research fellow at the Centre National de la Recherche Scientifique, affiliated with the Centre de Recherches Historiques at the École des Hautes Études en Sciences Sociales, Paris. Since 1988 she has regularly been a visiting professor in the Department of History at the University of California, San Diego. Giard's studies focus on the history of science and philosophy of the medieval and Renaissance periods. Michel de Certeau left Giard editorial responsibility for his works.